Finding Balance

Loving God with Heart and Soul,
Mind and Strength

Sisters
Bible Study for Women

Finding Balance

Loving God with Heart and Soul, Mind and Strength

Participant's Workbook

Becca Stevens

Abingdon Press / Nashville

SISTERS
FINDING BALANCE: LOVING GOD WITH HEART AND SOUL, MIND AND STRENGTH

Copyright © 2004 by Abingdon Press

Library of Congress Cataloging-in-Publication Data

Stevens, Becca, 1963-
    Finding balance, loving God with heart and soul, mind and strength / Becca Stevens.
        p. cm. -- (Sisters, Bible study for women)
    Includes bibliographical references and index.
    ISBN 0-687-34510-3 (binding: adhesive : alk. paper)
    1.   Women in the Bible--Meditations. 2.   Bible. N.T. Gospels--Meditations. 3.   Bible. N.T. Acts--Meditations. 4.   Christian women--Prayer-books and devotions--English. I. Title. II. Series.

BS2445.S74 2004
225.9'22'082--dc22

                            2004007860

04 05 06 07 08 09 10 11 12 13—10 9 8 7 6 5 4 3 2 1
MANUFACTURED IN THE UNITED STATES OF AMERICA

I would like to thank Angie Stephens, my patient and kind assistant,

and the leaders of St. Augustine's Chapel and Magdalene.

Thanks to Kelly Ayers, an intern from the Vanderbilt University

Divinity School, who helped get this project started;

and to Marcus, Levi, Caney, and Moses,

my family and the world's greatest teachers.

Contents

Introduction

It was a beautiful summer day when the folks from Abingdon Press arrived at my office to discuss the possibility of my writing a study for their Bible study series, *Sisters*.

"I can't do it," I said. "I have three kids, a church, and an organization to manage."

Although I wanted to write the study and felt it was a great opportunity to share some of my ministry insights from the past decade, I was afraid. What if I couldn't get it done? What if it wasn't good enough? Then it dawned on me that those fears and hopes were actually the seeds for the Bible study that I wanted to write for kindred women travelers along the Christian path.

For three months after agreeing to write the study, I wrote nothing. I simply let myself live with the doubts and hopes of my heart. First, I had to come to terms with my own inability to live faithfully with all of my heart, mind, and body. Next, I looked at what I wanted to say. Was it appropriate for a Bible study? I wondered about how to tell my husband that I had committed to writing a book. I worried whether I was capable of writing material that would offer women new insights, even though it felt authentic to me. For a long time, I fretted about how to incorporate my life and spiritual practices into a legitimate study of the Scriptures. One night while taking a long bath, I thought up legitimate excuses as to why my publisher should find a different writer. In spite of my worries, I knew that the book I wanted to write needed to be on the topic of a balanced life of faith.

I knew that I wanted to focus on how busy, capable, and faithful women come to terms with balancing faith and family. I knew that in order for any of us to have a sense of true inner peace, we must figure out how our *devotion to God* and *duty to others* can live in harmony. The women I admire have made their faith central to their daily lives. My problem then became how to develop a study that would bring women peace and insight, while doing the work of being more dutiful in their faith. My hope is that during the next six weeks *Finding Balance: Loving God with Heart and Soul, Mind and Strength* will help you draw closer to your Lord and give you peace as we explore the Scriptures together.

THE PATH OF OUR STUDY

The starting premise of *Finding Balance* is that all of us are capable of feeling overwhelmed, bored, guilty, and lost. Next is the assumption and assertion that the path that leads away from those feelings begins with prayer that is informed by our knowledge and love of God. One goal of this study is to remind us that we are the inheritors of a deep and abiding faith that can help us balance our duty and devotion and live in harmony. No matter where we find ourselves on the journey, our faith can bring us peace and assurance.

We can take comfort in knowing that women who have gone before us began laying down this path. They are our best guides as we try to live as deeply as we can into our faith. Over the next six weeks, we will look at how our foremothers have dealt with balancing duty and devotion in their lives of faith. By examining the Scripture lessons through the eyes of these women, we may see ways to journey more faithfully.

In addition to looking at women from the Scriptures, we will look also at women from history and women we know personally. Finally, we will turn to our own lives, to examine how we are called to balance duty and devotion. Throughout *Finding Balance,* we will use poetry, Bible stories, and reflection questions to help us begin a conversation about the crucial question: How do I live a balanced life of faith?

HOW TO USE THIS STUDY

Central to *Finding Balance* are the daily prayers that we will offer together, even though we are studying as individuals. These prayers are important because they are the answer to the question posed above. It is through prayer that duty and devotion are in communion. It is through prayer that we find our authentic voice, which will lead us to right service and right thinking. It is through prayer that we can search our hearts most honestly and find that place of union with God.

Introduction

I love the idea of prayer as the central piece to a women's Bible study, because the study of Scripture can provide the foundation for our connection to God, which we express in prayer. Although each of us prays in our own voice and has a unique life, our study of Scripture becomes a common thread that binds us. The study of Scripture brings us together so that we have a common starting place in our prayer life, a life as unique to us as our fingerprints. By starting with Scripture, we are reminded that we are part of a community, and not alone in our faith. We are part of a community of those who read the Scripture with us, and also have a relationship with God through prayer.

Our study will take place over six weeks, with each week based on a story about a woman or women from the New Testament. The six stories are Mary and Martha, Lydia, Mary the Mother of Jesus, the Canaanite Woman, Mary Magdalene, and the anointings of Jesus Christ. Each week will begin with the story; then, during the remainder of the week, we will use that story as a basis for reflection and prayer. I encourage you to read the Scripture story each day, or the text that is provided for that day, as a prelude to that day's reflection, thought, and prayer. In this way the Bible story will be exposed to many levels and perspectives of interpretation. I come from a tradition that celebrates the possibility of finding new meaning in old stories each time that story is engaged. The Scripture is a living word, and in quiet reflection God is revealed anew in our daily lives.

Each day, after studying the Scripture passage, the reading, and the reflection questions, allow yourself 15 minutes of silence. This quiet time is designed to allow an inner journey through the details of your own day, guided by your sense of God revealed. If you find the reflection questions a distraction rather than a launching point for reflection, ignore them. In most individual and corporate worship experiences, a space is included for silence. This silence is critical to the life of those on a spiritual journey. The study and thinking we do prior to our 15 minutes of silence is then offered to God, as a means of hearing God's voice through this study. Some may find silence to be the hardest part of the study to complete each day, but it can also be the most fruitful.

Finally, we conclude each reading with a common prayer. I am an ordained Episcopal priest who has worked side by side with a United Methodist pastor since 1995. During our service together, no matter what is going on, our common prayers have kept us on track and in communication with each other. Every week at our services we share in a *collect* (a special prayer) that is prayed by every congregation around the Anglican communion. We will follow this tradition as well. The prayers included in *Finding Balance* come from my heart and women and men of faith who are inspiring to me.

KEEPING A GRATEFUL HEART

I am thankful to be a part of the *Sisters* series. As a priest and a mother, I have asked myself the questions raised in this study for over a decade. While I don't have definitive answers, I have discovered ways of living that make my life more peaceful and connected. When I began a ministry to help women get off the streets, a ministry called Magdalene, my husband said, "You can't do this. It's just too much."

I wanted to respond that I felt I *had* to do it, that everything else would work itself out. Instead, I became defensive, assuring him that not only could I do it, but I would also be so organized that I could finish all of my work and still be able to pick up the children after school every day. Of course, I never got *that* organized; and my husband Marcus has always jumped in to help in a million ways. Still, I've learned that no matter what I take on in ministry, somehow it all gets done.

I still have doubts, nevertheless, as I take time to write this study. I pray that someday I will learn not to worry, or to wonder, *If I take time for what is important, will everything else follow?*

Early in my ministry, I met a women with eleven children. A Catholic, she went to Mass every morning. When I asked how she did it, she reflected, "When I make time for God, God makes time for everything else." I need to remember that observation as I try to serve each day in my ministry with my family, my church, and with the many women who are a part of Magdalene. Over the next six weeks, I look forward to sharing stories from these ministries and laughing at what a great teacher life continues to be for me.

I have always enjoyed sharing stories, especially about the people closest to me. When I have the ears to hear and eyes to see, they are indeed my greatest teachers. I have three sons, Levi, 12, Caney, 8, and Moses, 3. They speak the loudest to me when I think about how to balance my life. Just the other day Levi talked to me about prayer. He had been worrying a lot lately and prayed about it to God. Then he said, "God told me it was my problem, not his, but that he would be beside me while I worked it out." That prayer was mine as well as I wrote this series. It was my problem to get it done, but God was with me as I wrote it. This can also be our prayer as we face the challenge of balancing faith and the responsibilities of daily life. The following poem may help us remember where we have come from as faithful women.

The Motherline

We are the descendants of mothers,
Carried as a seed,
Sprouted from Eve's womb,
Naked and in need.

We chant like Abel's wife
Upon our first contractions.
"Lord, show us mercy in
your great compassion."

Rachel, Leah, Rebecca, and Sarah
Are where our begats begin
And how we count our lucky stars
That form our astral kin.

We sing the song of Hannah,
"Praise where the blessings flow"
and wonder at creation
and how our seed can grow.

We taste the salt of Deborah's tears
Who weeps by the window, alone
Crying out to our God,
"Where is my beloved son?"

We feel the hands of Martha
Who tended to your appointed
Who made ritual from duty
And with calluses was anointed.

We are their descendants
And give thanks and praise to them
Knit within their blessed wombs
To serve our God again.

Week One: Mary and Martha

DAY ONE: THE DOING AND BEING OF OUR LIVES OF FAITH

Luke 10:38-42

Now as they went on their way, he entered a certain village, where a woman named Martha welcomed him into her home. She had a sister named Mary, who sat at the Lord's feet and listened to what he was saying. But Martha was distracted by her many tasks; so she came to him and asked, "Lord, do you not care that my sister has left me to do all the work by myself? Tell her then to help me." But the Lord answered her, "Martha, Martha, you are worried and distracted by many things; there is need of only one thing. Mary has chosen the better part, which will not be taken away from her."

The above passage is a good place to begin our study in search of balance for our lives of faith. It incorporates our understanding of duty and devotion, doing and being, the two sides we need for balance. When we focus on duty, we feel the need to be more devoted and contemplative. When we focus on devotion, we feel the need to be stronger and more committed to our duties. In this story, Mary embodies devotion, and Martha embodies duty. While all of us know that in reality we carry both a Mary and a Martha within us, this passage illustrates the roles that both duty and devotion play in our faith.

In the story Jesus was busy in his ministry when he arrived at Martha's home. Martha was the one who welcomed Jesus, while Mary is simply described as Martha's sister. Verse 40 explains Martha's problem and how she chose to handle it. Martha's problem was that she was distracted by many tasks, and these tasks led her to be frustrated with her sister. So she went to Jesus to get some justice.

15

Let's think for a few minutes about how busy we are with our daily tasks, and why we might find this frustrating. Have you ever uttered, "There is just not enough time in the day"? I have. A billion-dollar industry is devoted to time management products, including courses on how to better manage your time. Day planners, and now electronic organizers, help keep many of our lives on track. One of my goals for the year is to learn how to better manage my time so that I get more done in a day. I have even purchased a laptop, so that when I am not near my office computer, I can still get work done.

Time continues to elude us, even as we try hard to grab hold of it. No matter how fast our Internet connections, how many drive-through windows there are, or how much planning and organizing we do, we still long for more time. For me, the more I try to squeeze into my day, the faster the time seems to slip through my fingers. During the first weeks after my first baby was born, an older women visited me and said, "Enjoy it. It goes by so fast." I thought, *Not if I keep having to be up half the night.* Looking back after twelve years, I think both perspectives about time are right. Sometimes it goes by slowly, especially when we are doing the daily tasks of caring for our families. At other times, years seem to fly by, and we wonder where time has gone.

On a daily basis, the thing that frustrates me most is not accomplishing what I have to do, regardless of how fast or hard I work. Sometimes there is just too much to be done. It's especially hard when something happens in the morning that puts me behind for the rest of the day.

One day, I was scheduled to speak at a gathering of women about the outreach work that I do with Magdalene. One of the principles on which Magdalene is based is that we give to others based upon our gratitude for what God has done in our lives. For me this means that I volunteer my time as the executive director, and that the $400,000 operating budget is funded through private gifts with no strings attached. This is a great witness to the gospel truth that all we have belongs to God, and that we should give willingly to our brothers and sisters our time, treasures, and talents. This is how we live in the presence of God. I was basing my speech on the idea that although Jesus only had to travel about 150 miles to get to Jerusalem, the trip took three years because he kept helping people along the way. My message was that the most important ministry that we have may happen "along the way" instead of during scheduled meetings and planned encounters.

As I was headed out the door to deliver my speech, someone from my son's school called saying he had left his lunch at home and needed me to bring it to him. I was so frustrated with my son. It was fine for Jesus to have to go out of his way for strangers who were sick and lost; but my son knows better, and I had a lot to do. I drove over to the school in a bigger huff than Martha had probably been in. When I handed my son his lunch, he said he didn't think I was going to come and that he was very thankful. That was a humbling day, to say the least.

Even though I know that the way to preach and live the Christian faith is to take the long road and be generous with my time, talent, and treasures, I find I get irritated and feel that many of my tasks are a distraction from what it means to love myself, my neighbors, and God. When the doing and the being of our lives get out of alignment, we get into Martha trouble and become frustrated and irritated.

One of my biggest annoyances is when people come to the church that I pastor, make a big mess, and then leave without offering to clean up. I feel that they are devaluing me, or at least my time. This must be how Martha felt. I can well imagine that the group with Jesus came in and made a fairly sizable mess— bringing in dust from the road, throwing their cloaks and sandals on the floor, and leaving dirty dishes when they finished eating. They simply walked into her house and made themselves comfortable, even though she probably had a million things to do. I imagine she too wanted to relax and enjoy the company and teachings of Jesus; but in the buzz of guests and dinner preparations, she was just too busy. She thought, *If only Mary would see how busy I am and help me.* So she went to Jesus and asked him to tell Mary to help her. Instead Jesus said, "Martha, Martha, you are worried and distracted by many things; there is need of only one thing. Mary has chosen the better part, which will not be taken away from her."

It seems that Jesus understood Martha's need to get things done. He also understood Mary's need to be in communion with the divine. This is one of the important points of this story. *Martha couldn't hear the message of how to be a faithful disciple, because she was too busy trying to get everything else done.* So the question for us is: How do we maintain our full schedules, deplete our spiritual batteries, and feel loving and compassionate toward our sisters? The answer is, We can't. Jesus often retreated to the wilderness when his spirit was in need of rejuvenation. He recognized his need to replenish his spirit and energy in order to be effective in all that he was called to do.

Numerous examples of faithful women remind us of the need for prayer and quiet time, so that we can be with our children, tackle problems at work, be creative in our relationships, and be happy in our spirits. We do not love God well when we are emotionally, spiritually, and physically exhausted. Jesus is not telling us to abandon everything we have to do; he understands that these things are important. He did not tell Martha to stop working or caring for her house. He said that listening to his word was the better part. In this passage Jesus is teaching us to take care of our spiritual needs first, by taking the time to rest, relax, pray, or commune with God in whatever way helps us most.

Reflecting and Recording

When do you feel most like a "Martha"?

When do you feel that your spiritual batteries are depleted?

What things do you worry about on a regular basis?

Prayer

Gracious and loving God, thank you for your servants Mary and Martha. Give us the wisdom in the ordering of our lives that we can hear the call to sit and the call to serve. Teach us, Lord, to see your face in the faces of all those we serve today. Help us hear your call to sit and pray. Help us to make the time to serve you in all that lies before us. Amen.

DAY TWO: MARY AND MARTHA, SIDE BY SIDE

Let's take a few minutes to sit Martha and Mary side by side and look at what each can teach us about ourselves. Martha and Mary lived in first-century Jerusalem. We learn about them from the Gospel of Luke, which contains stories about women not found in any of the other Gospels. There are ten other stories about women: the raising of the son of the widow of Nain (7:12-17), the woman crying out from the crowd (11:27-28), the bent woman (13:10-17), the woman sweeping (15:8-10), the persistent widow (18:1-8), the women at the cross (23:27-31), and the stories of the women included later in this study. These glimpses into the lives of women make this Gospel especially important to us as we try to understand our experience as women and find insight into our particular journey as disciples.

These stories, looked at together, illustrate a larger message that Luke wanted to offer the early church community: that women, while restricted in their roles and leadership, were involved in forming the identity of Christianity. They were also part of the proclamation of the good news, and Jesus often defended and praised women when they demonstrated their faith publicly. This is what he did for Mary in the story of Mary and Martha. In the face of an all-male inner circle, he defended Mary's right to sit at his feet and listen to the message of discipleship. The story can make us feel uncomfortable if we think of it as pitting sister against sister, or that we have to choose a side. Instead, it is good to remember that Mary and Martha are well remembered by the early church in the Gospel of John. Here they are beloved by Jesus and not in any disagreement with each another (John 11:1-45; 12:1-8). By looking at them as sisters, both of whom were capable of great faith and great work, they each have a good deal to teach us on this journey.

Martha's duty is a common theme in our lives as women. We can imagine Martha with an apron around her waist, hair tied back, just a little worn out and scurrying around the house trying to get her many tasks done. Have you ever stopped and counted the tasks you perform on a daily basis? In preparing this session, I tried counting mine one morning. Between taking the dogs out and helping finish up math homework, I had completed about twenty-five tasks before nine o'clock. I decided to stop counting when I realized it was making me tired. There is much more to duty than running in circles and being distracted.

The word in the text that is used to describe Martha's "work" translates in Greek as "service." (The word is *diakonia*, which later came to be a technical term referring to eucharistic table service, proclamation, and servant leadership.) "Martha served." This statement is usually passed over quickly in John's account, but how powerful it is! Service is extremely important as an expression of our faith. We are called to feed the hungry and clothe the naked as well as prepare the church for worship. It would be irresponsible to interpret the passage as meaning Christian service is trivial. The New Testament as a whole is a call to action, urging each of us to use our individual talents, to go out and simply "serve." Martha's role continues to be central to the ministry of our churches today.

Mary's devotion is presented as the counterbalance to duty. We can all imagine Mary on the floor with her hair flowing over her shoulders, leaning to one side as loving words pour into her soul. In biblical times, social norms dictated strict gender roles, so Mary should have been helping Martha. Instead, she sat and communed with Jesus. Jesus even said that Mary had chosen the better part. This idea was extremely radical for the time and illustrates the liberating message that Jesus brought the world. Not only was Mary accepted as a part of the circle of disciples listening to Jesus, she was praised for her decision to commune with Jesus. That is what prayer is about. Sometimes the busier we get, the more we think that time for prayer is a luxury, not an essential element in our lives of faith. This passage serves as a reminder that Jesus is asking us to take time to be with him. In this passage, he is calling each of us to sit and listen to one another and to listen to our hearts.

Reflecting and Recording

What forms of service make you feel that you are serving Christ?

Why do you sometimes feel better when you are busy, rather than simply being?

Prayer

O God, my heart is the gate to your Kingdom. Search me out and know me once again. Cleanse me through and through so that I can serve you faithfully and love you perfectly. Then rekindle the flame of passion in my heart to reach out to the world in love. Amen.

DAY THREE: CONTINUING TO WALK IN MARY AND MARTHA'S FOOTSTEPS

Luke 10:25-28

Just then a lawyer stood up to test Jesus. "Teacher," he said, "what must I do to inherit eternal life?" He said to him, "What is written in the law? What do you read there?" He answered, "You shall love the Lord your God with all your heart, with all your soul, and with all your strength, and with all your mind; and your neighbor as yourself." And he said to him, "You have given the right answer; do this, and you will live."

The above Scripture, known as the Summary of the Law, is contained in various forms in all four books of the Gospels. It reminds us that not only were the disciples and the early Christians called to love God with their whole being but also anyone today who wants to be God's disciple. We are called to love God in this special way. This is why we study the Scripture, pray, and serve one another, all in the name of love. Let's spend this day thinking about modern-day women who, like Mary and Martha, teach us what it means to love God well.

The following three women are examples for us to consider. All of them learned on their journeys what it meant to love God with their whole being. They learned to love God, maybe not in perfect balance, but at least in utter devotion and untiring duty to others. These women have influenced my life of faith and call me to try harder to offer my whole heart to God.

Dorothy Day died in 1981 after working in the Houses of Hospitality for over fifty years. She was the founder of the Catholic Worker Movement that began in the Bowery of New York. I visited the chapel where she prayed for all those years and was moved by the lack of great statues or silver chalices bearing her name. It was her love of God that made her so remarkable. She was a faithful woman whose duty and devotion to the poor made her a saint in the twentieth century. She knew that duty and devotion are inexplicably tied to service for the poor and that there is no better way to love God. Dorothy Day wrote:

> If everyone were holy and handsome, . . . it would be easy to see Christ in everyone. But it was not Christ's way for Himself. . . . Ask honestly what you would do, or have done, when a beggar asked at your house for food. Would you . . . give it on an old cracked plate, thinking that was good enough? Do you think that Martha and Mary thought that the old and chipped dish was good enough for their guest? . . . It is not a duty to help Christ, it is a privilege.

Catherine of Siena lived in fourteenth-century Italy. At eighteen she became a nun and began to live in solitude and silence, going out only for church. She illustrated devotion at its highest degree. At twenty-one she returned to her family and vowed to spend the rest of her life serving the poor. It was out of devotion that the greatest duty to others called her. Even as she served everyone in love, from the poor to popes, she maintained a deep inner life of devotion to God.

Catherine of Siena wrote that we are foolish and blind when we choose to cross through the water when the road has been built for us! The road she referred to is the path where duty and devotion live in unity within us and enable us to worship God and love our neighbor with our whole hearts. "This road," she wrote, "is such a joy for those who travel on it that it makes every bitterness sweet for them, and every burden light."

Many who knew and loved her considered **Mary Catherine Strobel** a modern-day saint who lived in Nashville, Tennessee. Her son, the Reverend Charles Strobel, speaks about his mother's work with admiration and love:

> Momma's response to duty came from a grateful heart. Her own mother died when she was just eighteen months old, and her father died when she was sixteen. She was widowed when she was thirty-eight and was left to raise four children under the age of eight. She never forgot how much she had received in life from others. "People don't have to be kind to you," she often said. Her elder relatives recall that even as a little girl she took food to her neighbors who were in need. From those

early days until she was tragically murdered in 1986, her devotion to others—the elderly shut-in, the homeless beggar, the grieving mother, the sick patient, the inconsolable friend—was her duty. And her duty was always her devotion to others. Karl Rahner said that the perfect Christian state is one in which both duty and devotion are the same, and their experience is perfect joy. Everyone who knew Momma felt that sense of joy. So many considered her their best friend, and she had a great ability to connect people in relationship of kin and kind. Never a stranger in any gathering, rather she was at home among the influential as well as with the humblest poor.

Reflecting and Recording

Can you remember how you have served Christ sparingly?

Can you remember serving others generously and the feelings you had about that service?

How can you serve your neighbor in the way that Dorothy Day, Catherine of Siena, and Mary Catherine Strobel served others?

Prayer

Grant us, gracious Lord, the privilege to offer our very best to you. Make our hearts big and our spirits generous. Keep us fueled by the miracle of love and time so that the more we offer to you, the more we have. Amen.

DAY FOUR: SERVICE AND SOLITUDE

Luke 11:27-28

*While he was saying this a woman in the crowd raised her voice
and said to him, "Blessed is the womb that bore you and the breasts
that nursed you!" But he said, "Blessed rather are those
who hear the word of God and obey it!"*

This passage from Luke illustrates the juxtaposition of prayer and service for women when they try to be faithful. Who is right, Mary or Martha? We would love to believe that we can choose. Do you want to be the woman with the broom or the woman in prayer? Our faith, however, tells us that we *cannot* choose. We have to be both. Service is an extension of our faith, and prayer fuels that faith.

There is a great story about a nun washing dishes at a convent. A woman enters the kitchen and asks when the prayer service is going to begin. The nun says, "Amen," as she finishes cleaning the plates. She turns to the woman and says that the prayer service has ended, but the woman is welcome to come back after dinner and begin with her again. When we pray, we are serving our Lord; and when we are serving, we are praying with our Lord. Jesus tells us that we are the most blessed when we hear the word of God and keep it. The way that we keep the word is to love ourselves, God, and our neighbors.

One conclusion we can draw from the study of Mary and Martha is that in a balanced life there is a place where duty and devotion meet. It is when we are in conversation with Jesus. He is the common thread between Mary and Martha, and he is our common thread in this endeavor to learn how to serve him with all our heart and soul, mind and strength. There is no better way to learn how duty and devotion can help us live a balanced life of faith than by learning to pray and studying the Scripture. Today's text reminds us that until we learn and keep the laws in our hearts, we cannot apply the lessons of the Gospel to our lives.

There are many ways for us to pray the Scriptures. Our daily silences constitute the practice of *contemplative prayer,* which means that after all the reading and work is completed, we set everything aside and in silence allow God to speak. In praying mantras, a line from Scripture is repeated again and again, such as: "Lord have mercy on me, a sinner." A practice, *lectio divina,* emerged in the late Middle Ages. It involves choosing a Scripture verse and reading it. First, a simple and practical verse is chosen. Then, the prayer is begun. One recites the short verse while in prayer. The idea is to learn what the passage means to you in God's presence and to embrace what feels like the truth of it in communion with God. The passage can be recited over and over or whispered silently while listening as the prayer speaks to you.

In my life, this prayer works best when I can be completely alone for at least thirty minutes. Often I have had to get into the bathtub and turn off the lights. Then in the quiet of my prayer, as I recite a selected passage, I am led to a new place. Many times I leave the prayer with a new outlook on a problem, or I feel completely relaxed and ready to face the rest of my day. I love the times when I read a passage and, though I have read it many times before, it seems brand new. I hear it from a new perspective or notice a word that I never knew was there.

All these practices of praying the Scriptures teach us that we are truly studying the living word of God. The Holy Spirit is present in the solitude, in the reading and praying of Scripture. This gives us the energy to go back into the world in peace to love and serve the Lord. Without a disciplined life of prayer based on the Bible, we feel worn out by our acts of service and burned out by the world's demands.

Reflecting and Recording

Is it harder for you to rest and see your rest as service, or to pray while you are working?

Prayer

Loving God, thank you for making us the body of Christ. Help us always to remember that we are your hands, your feet, your eyes. Teach us to use our hands to heal, our feet to serve, and our eyes to see you in all that we do. For the sake of Jesus, who offered his body for us. Amen.

DAY FIVE: GOD LAUGHS WITH US

Luke 12:22-23

He said to his disciples, "Therefore I tell you, do not worry about your life, what you will eat, or about your body, what you will wear. For life is more than food, and the body more than clothing."

All this talk about service and solitude leads me to remember a place halfway around the world, in a jungle in Ecuador, where I saw a woman in the most complete solitude possible.

I was traveling with a group on a mission trip, and we had taken a break from our drive through a forest in the Andes. We had stopped for lunch. Our van was parked by a gravel road with an old stone fence that protected us from the steep drop just past the shoulder. We walked around, stretching our legs and trying to take in the dramatic scenery of steep hills floating in the midst of clouds. I leaned over the small stone wall, and there she was, hanging clothing over a tree limb in front of a small bamboo hut that appeared to be carved from some of the thickest forest I'd ever seen. The hut was quite a distance from the road, across a valley and part of the way up the mountain facing us. There were no visible paths leading to her hut nor were any other huts within sight. There was only the woman and a forest full of trees.

I watched her move, trying to imagine how she got there and what she did during endless days and nights with no electricity. A question crept into my head: If a woman is alone in a forest and laughs but no one hears it, does she really make a noise? The question wove its way into my heart and touched one of my fears. I continued to watch the woman, realizing that somehow her presence was of great importance to me. I realized that it was part of a larger question: If a person lives her life without success, without fame, without fortune, without even a witness, does it have meaning?

I knew the answer was yes, but that didn't stop the question from frightening me. How would you or I make meaning in our lives living completely alone in the wilderness? How do we make our lives meaningful, knowing that we are not so different from that woman? Maybe I cling to Martha because I want to feel that my life has worth and meaning. Maybe I fear that if I sit like Mary, my life won't have value to others, and I will begin to wonder what its true worth really is. Maybe I worry about my life because sometimes I forget that life is more than the food we eat, the clothing we wear, and the amount of money in our paychecks.

I learned from that woman that when a tree falls in the forest, it always makes a loud noise. God, who created the tree and loves the world enough to give up a son for it, will always hear it. In fact, there is so much meaning in that woman's life that she spared a bit for me. I will never forget her, or all that she taught me about what real duty and devotion consist of when we are alone before God's eyes. Life is more than the sum of our parts; it is the journey of our hearts that began with God and returns to God.

Reflecting and Recording

What would your life mean if you weren't so busy?

What do you think is the most meaningful part of your life?

Prayer

My Lord and my companion, thank you for all the people in my life whom I love. Thank you for the moments of peace and the companionship of prayer. Strengthen my heart for the times of solitude, so that I may not grieve silence but celebrate the joy of time with you. Amen.

DAY SIX: GOD'S SERVANT

My mother was a Martha for sure. I have always thought that when I see her again in heaven, she will have gotten all the angels busy instead of just lying around playing those harps. She was a person who woke up the family early on Saturday morning by running the vacuum cleaner. She was a living testimony to the strength of Martha. One phrase she used frequently as we were growing up was, "Don't dilly-dally." It meant that it was unacceptable for us to sit around and waste time.

That voice still lives in my head, so I have a hard time doing nothing. It is okay to go to church, but somehow it is harder just to sit on my bed quietly and pray. It is okay to go on a hike for exercise, but it feels awkward to stroll down the street aimlessly. Part of what I have come to love in the passage about Mary and Martha is that both women got to have a conversation with Jesus. My mother, though, makes me feel a bit partial to the Marthas of this world. I have an image of my mom as Martha, whipping everything into shape and having enough food even if Jesus had brought more friends. When Martha realized that her sister wasn't going to work, she asked Jesus to tell Mary to get up and help. Marthas, like my mom, teach us great lessons about our faith.

One image I carry of my mom is of her standing in front of St. Luke's Community Center. For twenty years she was the director of that agency, which served about 200 neighborhood kids and helped house the homeless and feed homebound folks. One morning about 5:30, the part of the building that had just been renovated caught fire. When we arrived, there were fire trucks, cameras, and people hauling boxes out of the building. My mom stood there, visibly shaken, and started making a list of things to do to keep the project going. Only a Martha could pull that off with grace.

My mom died several years ago, and never once did I question whether she would be able to get something done; the only question was how. The year before she died, she raised over a million dollars to help build a beautiful sports and recreation facility. That building was more sacred to her than any cathedral. It was beautiful because it was practical, fun, and useful for the children. She taught us that the world is good; families are only as rich as their love; Kmart is a godsend; anything can be lost, so remember everything; a car's only value is to transport you; and children are angels.

All of these memories remind me that we are given a finite amount of time in this world, and how we use it is one of our best offerings to God. It is good to use our time and talents to the best of our ability to honor all of the gifts that we have been given, and it is good to lavish ourselves with time for prayer and study so that we know what it is that we have to offer. A favorite passage that reminds me of this is Luke 17:7-10:

> Who among you would say to your slave who has just come in from plowing or tending sheep in the field, "Come here at once and take your place at the table"? Would you not rather say to him, "Prepare supper for me, put on your apron and serve me while I eat and drink; later you may eat and drink"? Do you thank the slave for doing what was commanded? So you also, when you have done all that you were ordered to do, say, "We are worthless slaves; we have done only what we ought to have done!"

The best that we can hope for after serving God for our whole lives is to be thought of simply as servants, doing our duty.

Mary and Martha were two women whom Jesus encountered in his travels. He had already appointed the seventy to go out and serve and had just finished preaching about the good Samaritan. His whole ministry teaches us what it means to serve one another and how serving honors God. The passage after the story of Mary and Martha is Jesus teaching his disciples how to pray the Lord's Prayer. The lessons from these passages are designed to teach what discipleship and service mean. We are to apply these lessons to our daily tasks and in all our encounters, with hope that living out these lessons will bring us closer to the heart of God.

Reflecting and Recording

When do you feel like you have the most time?

If you walked into your kitchen and it was dirty, and on the table was a Bible and a broom, which one would you pick up and why?

Prayer

Lord, keep us faithful in our duties, watchful in the night, and steadfast in our devotion so that we can grow in our love for you all the days of our lives. Amen.

DAY SEVEN: PREPARING FOR GROUP DISCUSSION

Using the reflections and the readings, think about ways in which the silence is working for you, and about a story that demonstrates why you identify more with Martha or Mary. Why do you think most women will probably identify with Martha, not Mary? Then, take time to remember a Scripture that reflects how you bring your heart and mind into your daily practice of faith.

I wrote the following poem after an experience of calling for a minute of silence during a church service. I could hear the people rustling around, even as they tried to sit and pray in silence.

There is a restlessness filling this space.
Silent prayers are halted in mid-air
By the heavy sounds of uneasiness
Voiced in books scraping against wooden pews,
Rustling paper, cough, and shuffling shoes.
I hear my heart beating in my ears.

There is a restlessness hanging in the air.
A thick fog of doubt settles over the silence,
Causing the faithful to look around,
Tear out a check and rearrange their skirts.
I feel an itch just under my eye.
There is a restlessness stirring in my soul.
It's pulling me from the dreamy sleep

Of familiar tunes and my babbling speech:
"Dwell beyond this space and noise;
Cut through the fog and hear God's voice,
So in bright and lighter air you soar."

Week Two: Lydia

DAY ONE: A DEALER IN PURPLE CLOTH

Acts 16:13-15

On the sabbath day we went outside the gate by the river, where we supposed there was a place of prayer; and we sat down and spoke to the women who had gathered there. A certain woman named Lydia, a worshiper of God, was listening to us; she was from the city of Thyatira and a dealer in purple cloth. The Lord opened her heart to listen eagerly to what was said by Paul. When she and her household were baptized, she urged us, saying, "If you have judged me to be faithful to the Lord, come and stay at my home." And she prevailed upon us.

It is appropriate to begin our second week of study by moving to the second volume of Luke, called Acts. Acts is the book that tells the story of the church that began in the Gospel of Luke. Acts is also an amazing tale of Paul and Peter's journey and offers wonderful insight into the life of the early church, though it gives only limited insight into the role of women within the church. What we do get from the Book of Acts are some glimpses of women, their positions within the early church, and how they helped to form the unique community that became the church. It is important to remember, as we look to some of the women in Acts for guidance regarding how to live faithfully, that they lived in the male-dominated Roman world. Although there were a few women citizens who had wealth and enjoyed the social privileges of property ownership, most women were completely dependant on their husbands or on the owners of the households where they served. Full participation in

Roman culture, economics, and politics required wealth; and so all the women in Acts who are mentioned as supporters of the church were wealthy.

Another helpful piece of background information is that women were allowed only three roles of leadership in the early church. The first role was to use their wealth to support the disciples. Women could provide a place for the disciples to stay and could feed them and support their ministry. This was true of Lydia.

The second role was to provide care and food for the widows. This provision is described in 1 Timothy 5:16: "If any believing woman has relatives who are really widows, let her assist them; let the church not be burdened, so that it can assist those who are real widows."

The third role was as a prophetic minister. The best illustration is told in the story of Paul's visit to Philip in Acts 21:8-9, when Paul encounters the four unmarried daughters who had the gift of prophecy: "We [who were Paul's companions] left and came to Caesarea; and we went into the house of Philip the evangelist, one of the seven, and stayed with him. He had four unmarried daughters who had the gift of prophecy." So, with this brief bit of background, let's look at what these women have to teach us about our faith.

Lydia is a wonderful example of balancing duty and devotion. She represents first and foremost a woman who is independent and a freethinker. Interestingly, her name means "uncertain." From the story in Acts we learn that she is independent enough to change her mind and make decisions for her household. We also know from the text that she was Paul's first convert. It is worth noting in the story that the apostles were sitting by the river talking to women about faith. This was daring and unconventional. Not only were the apostles outside the gates, they were freely sharing the most important and personal aspects of their life stories with Gentiles.

Lydia was a Gentile who worshiped the God of Israel. It is significant that she dealt in the sale of purple cloth, and as such was probably wealthy. Purple dye was considered a precious commodity, usually worn as a sign of nobility or royalty. The purple cloth she sold was said to be worth its weight in silver. Our passage says that the members of her household were baptized along with her; so she must have had servants, perhaps even relatives, living with her.

It is possible that Lydia was not actually the woman's real name. She was from Thyatira, which was formerly in the ancient kingdom of Lydia before it was incorporated into the Roman Province of Asia. Since Thyatira was still considered to be in Lydia, her name may have meant something like "the Lydian lady." Some commentaries suggest that the name of this Lydian lady was either Euodia or Syntyche, which are mentioned in Philippians 4:2.

After Lydia's conversion she invited the apostles to come and stay with her; because of independent women like Lydia, their ministry was sustained and missionaries were sent out. She was a key to the establishment and development of the church in Philippi, which was the principal city in the region of Macedonia (northern Greece).

This story is about one woman who was in the right place at the right time, with the right heart, and with the right attitude. God can do amazing things through men and women who are prepared to seek, follow, and be obedient to God's vision. The story reminds us about the ways in which God can use us in the middle of our days, in the middle of our lives, while we are carrying out our daily tasks.

The story also leaves us with questions: Why were women gathered together talking about faith? What happened to the rest of the women with Lydia outside the gates? Often the stories about the early church give us hints about a person, since the Scripture writers' primary purpose was to focus on the miraculous nature of Jesus' message and the founding of church communities by Paul. But in the few lines we are given about Lydia, we find enough to give us hope and inspiration about our own roles in the life of the church.

One woman, Lydia, who appeared at the right time and with an open heart, played a significant role in the life of the church. It inspires us to believe that we too, individual women with open hearts and willing minds, can play a significant part in furthering the message of the gospel. Lydia, sitting with other women outside the gate, listened to the message and was fearless in her response to God's love and mercy.

I love the fact that Lydia encountered Paul relatively early in his ministry. It appears that, although she was not a Christian, Lydia was a seeker of truth because she had joined a sabbath day prayer gathering. Paul and Silas joined the gathering, sat down, and spoke to the women. It may be that Paul explained something that made Lydia so attentive and responsive that she in turn was baptized, along with her household. Lydia demonstrated boldness, courage, and generosity as she opened her heart and home to these strangers. As a business woman (a dealer in purple cloth), Lydia may have been a leader in the gathering, and so Paul may have paid more attention to her. As a businessman (a tent-maker), Paul may have found a common language to use with Lydia.

By sitting down with the women, Paul entered into a conversation; he was not just speaking to them but with them. He was able to recognize their deep spiritual needs, and he acknowledged Lydia's hospitality and enthusiasm. In this encounter, Paul demonstrated the strong leadership qualities of listening, encouraging, sharing, entering into dialogue, and accepting others, especially Gentile women. Paul did not appear to have imposed himself on this gathering; otherwise it is unlikely that Lydia would have been so ready to listen and believe what he said. The Lydias around us provide models that show, once again, that it is good for women to think on our own.

Reflecting and Recording

Am I, are you, the right woman, in the right place, at the right time, with the right heart, with the right attitude ready for God to use?

Can you imagine changing the course of your life to further the gospel message?

Have you ever felt called to a particular ministry in your life that you felt unable to fulfill because you are a woman?

Prayer

Thank you, God, for the path before us. Give us the courage to take the next step ahead and never to turn back. Amen.

DAY TWO: THE VISION OF LYDIA

1 Corinthians 11:5

*Any woman who prays or prophesies with her head unveiled disgraces her head—
it is one and the same thing as having her head shaved.*

One of the most hopeful things about reading the Acts of the Apostles and the
Letters of the early church is that we see women as having a prophetic voice and
being capable of sharing Jesus' vision for a new Kingdom. While the women are
restricted by the customs and norms of their cultures, it is clear from this passage
in Corinthians that they indeed are prophesying, even with their heads covered.

If that is true for Lydia and the other women, then it is true for us as well.
God's living word is still being written on our hearts. We still need to make our
lives open to the possibility that God will use us where we are, and because of
who we are, to proclaim the good news.

Occasionally we are graced by moments when the clouds part and we glimpse
the Ancient One, the Beloved, the Holy One in our midst. The church has tradi-
tionally called these glimpses visions. I believe that visions are really sight with
grace. The purpose of our visions is to gird us on our journeys of faith and bind
us again to our Lord. Visions serve to inspire us to be faithful in our duties and be
renewed in our devotion. There are stories of visions of the disciples, of our fore-
fathers and mothers, of the apocalyptic writers of Scripture, and of people we
know who see signs in nature and in dreams. The stories of Lydia and the other
women who were present at the beginning of the church are filled with visionary
moments that are exciting to read about. They serve to remind us that our God is

a living God who moves in us and in our churches. They remind us that it is the Holy Spirit that is leading us to be faithful and guiding us in our daily lives.

In the story of Lydia, the Holy Spirit guides Paul to Philippi and to Lydia. It is amazing to think that the church of Philippi was begun through a vision from the Holy Spirit that was given to Paul. Women, leaders like Lydia, used their inspired vision for the church. Without their vision and courage the church may not have been able to continue and grow through those incredibly hard and dangerous first two centuries. Their efforts have persisted to the present day, when what we see is the remnant of those visions in the places where we worship.

I have always treasured moments of vision in my life. I take these moments seriously, setting aside time to be in silent prayer and wait. One morning I got up around four o'clock to watch the shooting stars. Quietly I went out and looked up into a hazy sky, focusing on the tiny celestial bodies that were emerging. Moments later, my three-year-old, who had heard me shut the back door, joined me. He sat in my lap, asking again and again where the shooting stars were. That morning I learned that there is not enough time between seeing a shooting star and lifting your arm to point and say, "Look!" Each time I saw one, he missed it; and the best I could do was to give him a description. I told him we would try again when the night came, but that he would just have to keep looking and waiting; at some point he would surely see one of his very own.

The author of Ecclesiastes says that we will see visions and dream. All of us possess the ability to see a vision of God manifested in this world, but we cannot wait for others to point it out. By the time they raise their arm to show us, it is gone. We have to see our own vision. We must be faithful in believing that such a vision is possible in a world where it is unbelievable.

Jesus tells us over and over that if we have ears to hear and eyes to see, we will notice signs of the Kingdom all around us. Lydia teaches us to be open and ready for the visions in our lives. Surely vision is the place in the seam where the clouds are parting, where duty and devotion are blurred by absolute love.

Reflecting and Recording

Have you ever seen a vision? How did you know it was God?

Why do you think visions from God often come to us through dreams and in nature as well as through other people and reading Scripture?

Prayer

Holy and life-giving Spirit, give us the eyes to see and the ears to hear you at work in the world around us. Thank you for sight filled with grace in the sacred spaces of our prayers. Amen.

DAY THREE: SIX WAYS LYDIA BALANCED DUTY AND DEVOTION

Acts 16:37-40

Paul replied, "They have beaten us in public, uncondemned,
men who are Roman citizens, and have thrown us into prison; and now
are they going to discharge us in secret? Certainly not! Let them come
and take us out themselves." The police reported these words to the magistrates,
and they were afraid when they heard that they were Roman citizens;
so they came and apologized to them. And they took them out and asked them
to leave the city. After leaving the prison they went to Lydia's home;
and when they had seen and encouraged the brothers and sisters there, they departed.

As we said earlier this week, Lydia was the first official European convert that Paul met at the Philippian sabbath gathering of women. Paul met other women leaders in his travels and named several of them in the Book of Acts and in his Letters. When Paul talked about Priscilla, for example, he spoke of her in equal terms with her husband, as a leader and missionary in the church.

I am filled with admiration for these women who were willing to risk their lives for the sake of the gospel. They are our models, these first women believers. It is worth our effort to spend time reflecting on the qualities these women possessed, to see what we can glean for our own lives so that we can live a balanced life of head and heart, duty and devotion.

1. **Lydia was a woman of prayer.** When Paul encountered her, she was at a gathering for prayer. In Jewish law a synagogue could be formed wherever

there were ten male heads of households who could be in regular attendance. Failing this, a place of prayer under the open sky and near a river or the sea was to be arranged. Apparently there was no synagogue in Philippi. Paul had been there a few days and was looking for a place to worship. This explains why he and his companions went a little way out of the city to the river and expected to find a place of prayer.

2. **Lydia listened.** From the story we find out that she was eager to learn. At these prayer gatherings, teaching and knowledge were shared. It's significant that Acts 16:14 says, "The Lord opened her heart to listen eagerly to what was said by Paul." Imagine Lydia sitting there as she absorbed all that Paul was saying. What she heard was different from anything she had heard before. This was about a real person, Jesus. Paul said that Jesus was the long-awaited Messiah, who had been crucified to take away her sin, who had risen from the dead on the third day, appeared to the disciples, and then ascended into heaven. Paul may have even talked about his own dramatic conversion on the road to Damascus. Lydia listened, and her heart was touched by the message of the gospel. As well as being eager to learn, she was quick to respond.

3. **Lydia was a worshiper.** She was eager to pray, listen, and be a part of a gathering of women. Lydia is spoken of as a "worshiper of God" and so would have received instruction at a synagogue in her native Thyatira. In the prayer gathering by the river, the women would have been reciting prayers and reading from the Law and the Prophets. They would have discussed what they had read and what they hoped to hear from a traveling Jewish teacher who would bring an exposition or exhortation. Lydia had been worshiping God in the only way she knew. She was faithful; yet she did not understand whom she was worshiping. After opening her heart to the Lord, she could worship in spirit and in truth.

4. **Lydia was willing to open her heart.** When the truth was spoken, she was willing to believe. This is a simple statement, yet so significant. As Jesus often said, too many hearts are closed, hard places. As Lydia sat listening to Paul, the Holy Spirit was melting her heart, softening it to respond to Paul's message; and Lydia would never again be the same. That is what

happens when God touches us: hard hearts melt. It is why, again and again in the Gospels, God asks us to love with our whole hearts. The significance of stories from the Acts of the Apostles is that hearts, not minds, were changed. After those hearts were changed, there was no stopping the church from growing and the truth of the Gospels from being shared.

5. **Lydia was obedient.** She did what was needed to follow the message of Jesus given to her by Paul. Lydia, along with her household, was willing to be baptized. In biblical times, baptism followed closely after conversion. Then, as now, baptism is a symbolic way of burying your old life and rising up to take on the new life God has for you. Following her conversion and baptism, Lydia wanted to serve her fellow Christians. She had received something special and wanted to give something back. Often this happens when people become Christians. It is part of what makes them stand out; they have undergone a dramatic change that people notice. A changed life is one of the most powerful testimonies we can give. Knowing Jesus, learning about him, following him, becoming more like him involves a desire to serve as he did.

6. **Lydia was hospitable.** It is significant that the theme of hospitality comes up in numerous accounts of people hearing and responding to the gospel. One way that Lydia served was by opening her home, since she wanted to enjoy fellowship with other believers. Lydia's house became a center of Christian outreach and worship in Philippi. The Book of Philippians describes how the church had grown and what a special place it held in Paul's heart. As we read the end of Paul's encounter in Philippi, we learn in Acts 16:40 that Lydia's home was open to followers, even those fresh from prison! She practiced hospitality—not just when she felt like it, but when it was needed.

These six characteristics lay a steady foundation for our faith. If we are prayerful, listen to God, worship God, remain open to God's word, live in obedience, and show hospitality, surely we will be able to live with our whole hearts and minds dedicated to God. At times the task seems impossible. But Jesus provides hope, when he says that nothing is impossible for those who love God. Whenever we are trying to live out these virtues, we are growing closer to God.

I am thankful for the leadership and faithfulness of women such as Lydia, Priscilla, and the countless others whose names are never mentioned, thankful for the costs they paid so that the faith could be passed to us. Throughout our study, we must remember the many men and women who gave their lives in the name of faith. Our sacrifices pale in comparison.

Reflecting and Recording

How often do you go to a prayer meeting other than on Sunday morning in the sanctuary?

Have you ever listened to a message and known it was God speaking to you? Describe the experience.

Name one character trait that you share with Lydia.

Prayer

O God, you who have endowed us with a thirst that you alone can quench, a hunger that you alone can satisfy, and a restlessness that you alone can still, we turn to you in adoration and prayer. We turn to you because there is no one else to whom we can turn, confident of finding answers to our questions and quiet for our souls. Thank you, Lord, for the gift of the church and for your servant, Lydia. Amen.

DAY FOUR: PRISCILLA, LEADERSHIP, AND WOMEN

Acts 18:1-4, 18-19

Paul left Athens and went to Corinth. There he found a Jew named Aquila, a native of Pontus, who had recently come from Italy with his wife Pricilla, because Claudius had ordered all Jews to leave Rome. Paul went to see them, and . . . he stayed with them, and they worked together—by trade they were tentmakers. Every sabbath he would argue in the synagogue and would try to convince Jews and Greeks. . . . After staying there for a considerable time, Paul said farewell to the believers and sailed for Syria, accompanied by Priscilla and Aquila. At Cenchreae he had his hair cut, for he was under a vow. When they reached Ephesus, he left them there, but first he himself went into the synagogue and had a discussion with the Jews.

Lydia was a woman of wealth and influence. As the first European convert of Paul and the founder of her own church, she is to be taken seriously as an early Christian leader. There are many other women mentioned prominently in Acts. For example, Sapphira, the wife of Ananias, is described as having property and financial acumen. Tabitha, who in Acts 9 is described as a woman full of good works and charity, was raised by Paul. In Romans 16, Paul refers to Priscilla and Aquila as fellow workers in Christ Jesus. Priscilla and her husband were sent out with Paul as missionaries to Ephesus. Many biblical scholars call Priscilla the most prominent woman of the New Testament because she preached in several cities, and the Book of Corinthians hints that their home became a center of the church.

Many of the stories throughout Acts and the Epistles teach us that women were sentenced to jail as members of Christian communities and subjected to the same persecution as their male counterparts. Acts 17 tells us that the leading women who were converted were of high standing. In Romans, Paul says that Phoebe, a deacon of the church at Cenchreae, had helped him.

We can conclude from these references that women played a leading role in early Christianity by serving as ministers of the church. They were allowed to preach and pray in worship as well as to prophesy and teach. It was only after the church spread throughout Rome that it needed to consolidate its doctrine, and as a result women were given a less important role.

As a child growing up in the church, I thought I would love to marry a pastor. It wasn't until high school that I realized I didn't have to *marry* a pastor; I could be one myself. This was one of the most liberating moments of my Christian journey. I knew that women and men throughout the church had paid dearly so that women could be ordained in the 1970s. How sad it must have been for women before that time to want to be a priest and then have the church deny their wishes because of their gender. I am deeply grateful to be able to exercise my calling and not have to depend on someone else to fulfill my heart's desire. Unlike early women pastors, I have never been asked to apologize for feeling led to my calling, or to defend myself in light of particular Scriptures that restrict the role of women.

Surely part of the reason women feel out of balance in their faith is that they have been restricted from expressing themselves freely by the cultures in which they live. I celebrate that in my life I have the freedom to be a mother, preacher, and teacher. As women we should not feel that we have to do ministry the same way as our male predecessors. Instead we need to have options open to us, so that we can hear God's calling and answer that call when we feel moved.

Reflecting and Recording

When have you experienced the freedom of knowing that you can be whatever you want to be?

When have you been a model to encourage other women to think on their own?

Prayer

O God, who has proven Your love for all humanity by sending us Jesus Christ our Lord, and has illuminated our human life by the radiance of His presence, I give You thanks for this Your greatest gift.

For my Lord's days upon the earth:

For the record of His deeds of love:

For the words He spoke for my guidance and help:

For His obedience unto death:

For His triumph over death:

For the presence of His Spirit within me now:

I thank you, O God.

Grant that the remembrance of the blessed Life that once was lived out on this common earth under these ordinary skies may remain with me in all the tasks and duties of this day. Amen.

(from John Baillie, 19th-century theologian)

DAY FIVE: NO TURNING BACK

For almost eight years I have worked with women coming off the streets or out of jail. This ministry is the fruit of my life of prayer and a wonderful opportunity to serve God. I delight in the women's growth and successes and am willing to sit with them during their setbacks and hard times. Many of the women who have graduated from the program, gotten jobs, and are living on their own are still friends. The program, called Magdalene, currently has four houses and runs a cottage industry that helps women make the transition from being prostitutes and drug addicts to living as part of a community.

When Magdalene was begun, I had no idea how drastically the program would affect my life or how much work it would take. If I had known, I might never have opened the first home. The daily needs of the women can be overwhelming as can the pressures brought on by the fifteen staff members. Looking back, I am grateful that I could not see the future. The idea of running a half-million-dollar-a-year program solely on donations would have seemed like a hill too big to climb. Sometimes I believe that God simply gives us enough vision to see the next day and the faith to walk into it. It isn't until we have walked a long way that we can look back and think: Thank God, I had no idea how rich and how tiring this life of duty and devotion would be.

In the Gospel of Luke and the Acts of the Apostles, there are at least ten scenes of Jesus and his disciples retreating for rest and prayer during their ministry. It wasn't that they were *burned out,* which is a great term but is overused when applied to people in the helping ministries. It was that they were faithful and wanted to be able to keep loving the people whom they met along the way. It was that they needed to reflect on what had happened and have a chance to hear God speak to them again. Each of us is called to ministry for our *whole* lives, and often we cannot even imagine the places where we are called. So we keep working, and we keep retreating to prayer to hear again God's voice.

Each week as we strive to learn more about balancing our lives of faith, we will look at examples of faithful women from history. Last week we talked about Dorothy Day, Catherine of Siena, and Mary Catherine Strobel. This week we will look at Teresa of Avila and Sister Constance of St. Mary's Convent in Sewanee, Tennessee. Both Teresa and Constance are wonderful examples of how far a vision or idea can carry you in a life of faith, and how powerful faith can be in determining the course of your life.

Teresa of Avila was born on March 28, 1515. She entered the Carmelite convent of the Incarnation in Avila in 1536. Later, she would reform the order, bringing a part of it back to the stricter primitive rule. The first house of the reform was founded in 1562 and was followed by fifteen more houses before she died in 1582. This was a huge number of houses to oversee and make sure that the nuns were living by the established rule. She had enormous responsibilities as an administrator and as the spiritual leader of all the houses. One of her prayers was, "May His Majesty grant I may never go back and be lost!" It meant that it would have been difficult for her to return to where she began, because she had taken such a long and winding path. Teresa remained devoted to the work and to her Lord until her death. She said, "God always enriches the souls he visits. This is certain, for although the favor and consolation may pass away quickly, it is detected later on by the benefits it has left in the soul." She often spoke of the need for us to forgive others and be humble in prayer, as a testimony to God's treatment of us.

Sister Constance lived at St. Mary's Convent in Sewanee, Tennessee, in the late 1800s. Sister Lucy Shetters, current head of the convent, tells the story of Constance and her companions. Her telling is a witness to the power of Christ-like denial for the sake of others and the beauty that can be found in living in obedience to our call. Constance and a group of sisters from St. Mary's went to Memphis in 1873 to start a school for girls. Confronted by the yellow fever epidemic when they arrived, the sisters instead cared for the sick and dying. They finally opened the school but then faced an outbreak of the plague in 1878. While most people who could leave the city fled, Constance stayed and brought in new sisters to help the doctors. Within two weeks of that decision, Constance died, followed closely by the deaths of several doctors, clerics, and nuns. Courageous and tireless in their work, they became known as the "martyrs of Memphis."

Reflecting and Recording

What prayer do you pray most often—for strength to carry on your ministry or for God to show you a new path of service?

How can prayer change the work that you do?

Where do you think people like Constance and Teresa got their strength and courage?

Prayer

For all the saints, who in their nobility served you, I offer my deepest praise. For all my sisters who are instruments of your grace and mercy, I offer my deepest gratitude. Amen.

DAY SIX: LONELINESS IN ANOTHER KEY

One of the conclusions to draw from this week's study of women and the early church is that however we decide to practice our faith, it makes a difference. The choices we make will influence our future and the futures of those around us. Another conclusion that can surely be drawn is that choosing to believe will cost us our lives. That is, if we make choices based on our beliefs, our lives will never be the same. We lay down our lives and are offered new lives full of meaning, truth, and daily opportunities to love our neighbors.

We are also offered the freedom to follow our hearts with no apologies. The hard part, though, is that sometimes when we choose to walk in faith, the journey is lonely. As we spend this time weighing duty and devotion in our lives, we must be honest about just how lonely it can be. Almost every saint we could read about has mentioned this loneliness.

Therese of Lisieux, who was born in Normandy in 1873, wrote about "the night of the soul." She described it as a wall that reaches to the heavens and shuts out the starry sky.

> When I sing in my verses of the happiness of heaven and of the eternal possession of God, I feel no joy. I sing out of what I wish to believe. Sometimes, I confess a feeble ray of sunshine penetrates my dark night and brings me a moment's relief, but after it has gone, the remembrance of it, instead of consoling me, makes the blackness seem denser still.
>
> (*The Joy of the Saints: Spiritual Readings Throughout the Year*, Darton, Longman and Todd, 1988; page 16)

Despite her loneliness, Therese wrote that she would not have traded anything for the journey, and that in her longing she found mercy and sweetness.

Howard Thurman, a great theologian of the twentieth century, talked about a darkness that was like "loneliness in another key." It is the loneliness of the truth-seeker who searches beyond the familiar boundaries of life. As each one of us tries to be a truth-seeker in our faith, we may at times feel the loneliness Thurman describes. Lydia reminds us that it is only when we live into the truth of our lives, no matter where that carries us, that we are really being honest. If we, like Lydia, were to encounter a new truth, would we be brave enough to change?

One of the most poignant passages about the lifelong journey of faith comes from the Gospel of John, Chapter 21. The resurrected Jesus appeared to Peter and several other disciples on the beach. Jesus asked Peter three times if he loved Jesus, and three times Peter answered yes. Then Jesus turned to Peter and said:

> "Very truly, I tell you, when you were younger, you used to fasten your own belt and to go wherever you wished. But when you grow old, you will stretch out your hands, and someone else will fasten a belt around you and take you where you do not wish to go." (He said this to indicate the kind of death by which he would glorify God.) After this, he said to him, "Follow me."

Out of a passionate devotion and powerful sense of duty, Peter once again followed Jesus and shared the message of resurrection. We are called to live with that kind of passion and commitment. No one can make the commitment for us, and no one can know the cost of the decisions we make because of our faith. We can, however, walk with one another through the loneliness and burden of living honestly.

Often I have found comfort and joy in sharing stories with other women about the loneliness they have felt raising children and ministering to others. On those occasions, I have been reassured and have discovered that I am not lost. If you take only one thing away from this study, let it be a sense of encouragement to follow your heart, knowing there are others who share the cost, the loneliness, and the wonder.

Reflecting and Recording

Is there anything in your life that keeps you from making a full commitment to your life of faith?

Can you imagine that your faith would ever take you somewhere you didn't want to go?

Prayer

Almighty and eternal God, so draw our hearts to you, so guide our minds, so fill our imaginations, so control our wills, that we may be wholly yours, utterly dedicated to you; and then use us, we pray, as you will and always to your glory and the welfare of your people; through our Lord and Savior Jesus Christ. Amen.

DAY SEVEN: PREPARING FOR GROUP DISCUSSION

When you think about the early church, is it hard to imagine that women were prominent in its formation? When you think about your role in your church community, is it hard for you to imagine yourself in a leadership role? Does that give you more or less freedom to follow your heart in your life of faith?

This poem describes one of those perfect days of prayer for me.

Thick grey skies
Wrap dreary days,
Like leftovers to be tasted,
To see if they are worth saving.

Breaking through the wrapping,
Three hawks land in the magnolia tree
Slicing the grey with white bellies and bladed wings.

The creation, the creator, the created
More than one can fathom.
In majestic flight,
They transubstantiate.

Now grey is the curtain
For their joyful dance
Muted for tenderness.

Now grey is the paper upon which
Visions are painted by those
Who wish to fly to higher ground.

Week Three:
Mary, the Mother of Jesus

DAY ONE: THE EMBODIMENT OF DUTY AND DEVOTION

Luke 1:26-38

In the sixth month the angel Gabriel was sent by God to a town
in Galilee called Nazareth, to a virgin engaged to a man
whose name was Joseph, of the house of David. The virgin's name was Mary.
And he came to her and said, "Greetings, favored one!
The Lord is with you." But she was much perplexed by his words
and pondered what sort of greeting this might be. The angel said to her,
"Do not be afraid, Mary, for you have found favor with God.
And now, you will conceive in your womb and bear a son,
and you will name him Jesus. He will be great,
and will be called the Son of the Most High,
and the Lord God will give to him the throne of his ancestor David.
He will reign over the house of Jacob forever, and of his kingdom
there will be no end." Mary said to the angel, "How shall this be,
since I am a virgin?" The angel said to her,
"The Holy Spirit will come upon you,
and the power of the Most High will overshadow you;
therefore the child to be born will be holy; he will be called Son of God.
And now, your relative Elizabeth in her old age has also conceived a son;
and this is the sixth month for her who was said to be barren.
For nothing will be impossible with God."
Then Mary said, "Here am I, the servant of the Lord;
let it be to me according to your word." Then the angel departed from her.

Mary, the mother of Jesus, represents the highest form of duty and devotion through her witness in the Gospels. Beginning with the story of the Annunciation, through the Visitation, the presentation in the Temple, the flight to Egypt, the scene at the Temple when Jesus was twelve, the marriage feast and first miracle, and finally her presence at the crucifixion of her son, we are constantly made aware that Mary embodies a life fully given to God. She is mentioned more than any other woman in the Gospels and is revered for her place as the mother of the Incarnate Word of God. Mary has come to be considered equal with the disciples and the object of devotion for many faithful believers throughout the Christian tradition.

Before we delve into specific Scriptures about the mother of Jesus, let's remember that not all of the Gospels treat her the same way. We know that each Gospel has a different authorship and contains different material. They were written for different communities and had different goals for their theological teachings. In looking at Mary and what she can teach us about duty and devotion in faith, we need to remember that we see Mary through the lenses of the various writers of the Gospel. In Mark, for example, there is no infancy narrative; and when Jesus' family is brought into the story in Chapter 3, Jesus claims his true family as the people who do the will of God. Also in Mark, the shortest of the Gospels, is the story of the Son of God and those around him, who ultimately misunderstand the message he preaches of sacrifice and service.

Let's begin our study this week with the introduction of Mary in the Gospel of Luke. It is commonly believed that in this passage Mary is an unwed teenager and that conceiving a child would bring her and her family humiliation and disaster. Mary's response to the idea that she will bear a child has been echoed by women in every generation: "I'm what?" The idea is always startling to us, as we realize that our bodies and our lives will never be the same.

What sets Mary apart as a faithful and humble woman is her next response: "Let it be to me according to your word." It is this response to Gabriel that makes the conception possible and links humanity to God for eternity in an especially intimate way. From the beginning Mary was willing to be a servant of God. She saw in the birth of her son that God was exalting the lowly and scattering the proud, and that through him a heavenly Kingdom on earth was possible. God's love was made flesh through Mary, and it changed our world forever.

This story makes it clear that Mary belongs to the family of disciples. Like the disciples, she is a faithful servant of God who willingly goes where God calls her. When Mary realizes she is pregnant, she heads up into the hill country to be with her cousin. Together they sing the song of Hannah, about the glory of this new life. She acts as a faithful disciple by sharing the good news with others, such as Elizabeth. Mary's discipleship continues through the Gospel of Luke; she is even mentioned as being present at the Resurrection scene (Luke 24:1-10).

As we look at the figure of Mary, we must be mindful that some women feel that her adoration has hindered, not helped, those women who want to be leaders and teachers in the church. The reasoning is that the portrayal of Mary as being so perfect makes it impossible for the rest of us to live up to her example! So, we are left to feel less than worthy. Once while on a panel discussion, I sat next to a Catholic nun. The conversation concerned the role of women in the church for the past twenty-five years. The nun was asked about the adoration of Mary. Without missing a beat she said, "Mary is both the best and the worst thing for Catholic women. On one hand she is seen as equal to the disciples; but on the other hand, as a virgin mother she sets a standard that is impossible for the rest of us to meet." This was a particularly insightful and humble expression of our dilemma as Christian women. We all live somewhere between the two Marys: Mary, the virgin, and Mary Magdalene, the sinner from the street. How do we experience our lives of faith in that middle ground?

Reflecting and Recording

How does the example of Mary inspire you?

In what ways does the possibility of motherhood connect women to God?

Have you ever thought of Mary as one of the disciples?

Prayer

Holy God, unto whom all hearts are open, all desires known, and from whom no secrets are hidden, cleanse our thoughts through the inspiration of thy Holy Spirit, that we may perfectly love thee and worthily magnify thy holy name; through Christ our Lord. Amen.

DAY TWO: THE GIFT OF MOTHERHOOD
IN OUR LIVES OF FAITH

Luke 2:19

Mary treasured all these words and pondered them in her heart.

Let's spend a little more time thinking about the gifts of motherhood. Not all of us are mothers in the literal, biological sense. But all of us have experienced motherhood through our relationships with our parents, and many of us have "birthed" and nurtured ideas, plans, projects, and ministries that are dear to us. As we discuss biological motherhood, ponder the things in your own life that constitute or suggest the idea of motherhood.

Think about all the lessons you learned at the feet of your mother. Remember how you learned to look at the world partly through her eyes. See that in many ways our faith came to us because we were daughters and knew the love of our mothers, aunts, grandmothers, and other women who cared for us, before we could even say the word *God.*

As solid as those underpinnings may seem, for many of us the journey to our own motherhood has seemed precarious and frightening. Motherhood is a road that we take "ready or not," whenever our baby decides to come into the world. This is true whether the baby is a child, an idea, or a ministry.

Motherhood gives us some of the greatest insights into faith, humility, and femininity. It is where we learn that we are not in control of our own body, let alone another human. When a new baby is born, in some ways all we can really do is ponder the miracle of life as Mary did.

When my first two sons were born, I felt nervous about bringing them home. With my third son, Moses, I finally felt comfortable. I was keenly aware of how quickly the newborn phase passes and was cherishing every day that I got to hold him. I especially loved giving him baths.

One day as I bathed Moses, I was letting all my best and most hopeful thoughts for a good life wash over him as freely as the water. He was two months old, beautiful and round, healthy and strong. As I filled my hand with water once again, a thought crossed my mind: "Am I baptizing my son by accident?" If the act of baptism is the pouring of water over a child of God by a minister of the church with prayers of love, encouragement, and hope for eternal life, then the answer was a definite yes. In fact, by that time I had already baptized him at least twenty times! I laughed to myself, thinking how silly the idea was. "I'm just his mom," I said to no one. "I'm just giving him a bath."

With ideas of baths and baptism floating in my mind, I began a journey along the mother line, imagining the countless women who had baptized their babies with prayers and palms full of water. Alone with their babies, the mothers were free to celebrate and marvel at the special qualities of their children. I leafed through the pages of an imaginary photo album that showed generations of mothers bathing all sorts and conditions of babies: healthy babies, sick babies, crying babies, boys and girls of all races and creeds, each one perfect to the new mother whose heart is just mending and who naturally offers prayers of love as she washes the new skin.

I could see a mother in the Middle Ages, bathing a newborn daughter and then putting a home-tatted dress on her so the priest could come and pour a bit of water on her head, then wipe it off quickly as it began to drip. I could see a rural woman waiting for months for the itinerant preacher to come and then rushing to clean the baby so the prayers could begin and the feast commence. I could see myself running to the hospital to baptize a baby son who was dying, whose mother had already wept a river of tears on his forehead, giving him the most holy bath of all. I could see all those women, as the church offered the rite of baptism, beaming with pride and thankful that others had now joined in her silent prayers for her child.

In my heart I could see that I would dress my son in a beautiful gown and take him to the church to be blessed in front of the community that I love. I would introduce my son to the sacrament of baptism and keep bathing him with every good thing that I know. I wanted the community of faith to promise to love him and care for him. I promised God in that bath that I would bathe my son throughout his life, with handfuls of whispered prayers and kisses.

That experience of bathing my son was not unique. It was one of those times when we are present to the great gift of motherhood and the love we feel in birthing our children and our ideas. I don't ever want to forget that experience or want any of us to take it for granted, even if our children are grown and gone, even if our children are simply our hopes and dreams.

There are not many Scriptures in the New Testament that truly celebrate motherhood, so I love the image of Mary as mother, loving her son and treasuring her experience with him. I love the fact that in the greatest experience of God loving us and coming into the world, motherhood was central to the story, and that in all my life and learning, it has been through motherhood that I have found the mystery of life touching my heart and calling me to live anew.

Reflecting and Recording

What childhood memories do you have of experiencing God's love through your mother?

If you are a mother, how did you feel about yourself as part of creation at the time you gave birth to your first child?

If you are not a mother, think of a time when you were part of creating something. How did it make you feel?

Prayer

Gracious and loving God, we give you thanks for our mothers and our children. Thank you for teaching us how to love you through them and to see you in their faces. Thank you for making us part of your creation and for giving us the gift of life. Teach us to cherish it every day. Amen.

DAY THREE: THE MAGNIFICAT

Luke 1:46-55

And Mary said, "My soul magnifies the Lord,
and my spirit rejoices in God my Savior,
for he has looked with favor on the lowliness of his servant.
Surely, from now on all generations will call me blessed;
for the Mighty One has done great things for me,
and holy is his name.
His mercy is for those who fear him
from generation to generation.
He has shown strength with his arm;
he has scattered the proud in the thoughts of their hearts.
He has brought down the powerful from their thrones,
and lifted up the lowly;
he has filled the hungry with good things,
and sent the rich away empty.
He has helped his servant Israel,
in remembrance of his mercy,
according to the promise he made to our ancestors,
to Abraham and to his descendants forever."

The Magnificat is the hymn of gratitude for all mothers. It sings the praises of our creator who has graced us with the gift of motherhood. It celebrates how that gift erases all the injustices we find in this world. The hymn was first sung by Hannah when she found that late in life she was pregnant with Samuel (1 Samuel 2:1-10). Hannah sang, "My heart exults in the LORD; / my strength is exalted in my God. . . . / There is no Holy One like the LORD, / no one besides you." Mary picked up this hymn and, even though she was young and single, saw this gift from God as the greatest honor. My heart sings when she praises God, who has lifted up a lowly maiden and given hope to all those who are hungry and poor throughout the world. Standing in Mary and Hannah's shadows, I marvel at how they received God's blessing with no care for their own peace of mind or safety.

The Magnificat can strengthen us when we feel overwhelmed by the problems in the world. It can lift us when we think about the suffering of the poor and needy. It can inspire us when we ask the question, "What could I possibly do?" For the past five years, I have belonged to a group called the Daughters of the King. It is an interdenominational prayer group whose members have taken a vow to pray daily and be involved in service for others. We gather monthly in a member's home and begin with a prayer: "Lord, I am but one, but I am one. I can't do everything, but I can do something. What I ought to do, I should do. Lord, what would you have me do?"

The Magnificat rises from that same spirit. It calls us to believe that even in our smallness there is great potential. The Magnificat is mythical. Its beauty has inspired great composers and writers. Its prominence is demonstrated by its place as a central prayer in the rosary. It fills the Christmas season with mystery and sweetness.

I have always loved Mary's story and romanticized what it would have been like to be such a vessel of God's incarnate love. Once while eight months pregnant at Christmas, I felt close to Mary. But on Christmas Eve at two o'clock in the morning, my son kicked me hard in the kidney, waking me up with a gasp. My husband had already moved to the guest room, trying to give me a little more space and some relief from body heat. Wide awake, with a rare moment of silence in the house, I began to think about being very pregnant at Christmas, and how I should probably have insights into Mary's feelings, a special bond. Then my thoughts took a different course, and the images they conjured up were more like Scrooge than Mary.

The image of Christmas future was of an eleven-month-old boy screaming in a high chair, with strained peas dripping down his face. I hear a terrible crashing sound and know my older boys have decided to play Ninja and are leaping from an upper bunk in the room above me. I worry that the chandelier will fall on the baby and me. Calling out for the boys to stop, I set the baby down and run upstairs. I promise to play with the boys as soon as I finish feeding the baby, who in the meantime has crawled to the Christmas tree, which I hear toppling over.

In the darkest moment of the night, my doubts and fears about motherhood shame me. My heart tries to reassure my brain: *I am a joyful and thankful person who loves Christmas and my family. I just need to be less selfish and quit worrying.* I should have remembered the Magnificat, when in the midst of all her upheaval and wonders, Mary sings of being humbled and blessed and a handmaiden of the Lord. She ponders all things and welcomes all the problems. Do all pregnant women in the weeks before birth know the Magnificat is a call to motherhood?

On this Advent night, all my years of disciplined prayer and service don't give me comfort. I feel worried and selfish. I want to be full of expectation and joy. I want that wonderful feeling of excitement before the curtain opens, the joy of seeing a wrapped present with my name on it. I want to wake up in the morning and make a gingerbread house with my children and have the house smell of cloves. Instead, I feel guilt for how I have failed people and let Mary and all women down. I worry about money, about people in jail and on the street, about my children, about marriage and how to be in love when you have three children.

I want to praise Mary for the intimacy that the Incarnation offered the world. I lie awake dissecting the Nativity story and wonder how many people really understand the nature of the relationship of the Holy Spirit, Mary, and Joseph. Then, just as I am trying to imagine hosts of angels singing in the night to a field of shepherds, I hear the bells of the nearby university strike three A.M. Suddenly, the doubts and fears seem a little funny. Maybe when we hear a bell, it's not an angel getting its wings, like in the movie *It's a Wonderful Life*. Maybe it's God laughing as another of God's children discovers her own humanity.

I discover that my anxieties and doubts have left me—not broken or alone but thankful and joyful as the baby gives me another kick in the side. This baby, like all the babies of God, reminds me that we are left with love to ponder in our hearts like the beloved mother herself. And that love, emanating from within and generating heat and from without in the sound of bells, is enough. The love that is broken and tender is our connection to Mary. I imagine she had some of her own anxious moments while riding the donkey and thinking about labor; and I imagine Jesus did some roundhouse kicks of his own.

Reflecting and Recording

Have you ever experienced yourself as a vessel for God's redeeming acts of love in this world?

What acts of devotion do you find the most difficult to practice?

Prayer

O God, you have taken to yourself the blessed virgin Mary, grant that we, who have been redeemed by his blood, may share with her the glory of your eternal kingdom. Amen.

DAY FOUR: FOLLOWING IN HER FOOTSTEPS

John 2:1-11

On the third day there was a wedding in Cana of Galilee, and the mother of Jesus was there. Jesus and his disciples had also been invited to the wedding. When the wine gave out, the mother of Jesus said to him, "They have no wine." And Jesus said to her, "Woman, what concern is that to you and to me? My hour has not yet come." His mother said to the servants, "Do whatever he tells you." Now standing there were six stone waterjars for the Jewish rites of purification, each holding twenty or thirty gallons. Jesus said to them, "Fill the jars with water." And they filled them up to the brim. He said to them, "Now draw some out, and take it to the chief steward." So they took it. When the steward tasted the water that had become wine, and did not know where it came from (though the servants who had drawn the water knew), the steward called the bridegroom and said to him, "Everyone serves the good wine first, and then the inferior wine after the guests have become drunk. But you have kept the good wine until now." Jesus did this, the first of his signs, in Cana of Galilee, and revealed his glory; and his disciples believed in him.

Since the time of the earliest Christian communities, Mary has held a high place in worship, especially among Roman Catholics. She has been the source of strength for many suffering martyrs. There have been visions of her throughout the world, and people have brought loved ones to her for healing. In our Scripture today, Mary is the instigator for Jesus' introduction into public ministry. Mary and Jesus were at a wedding in Cana of Galilee, and during the reception she urged him to make everything right. Jesus told her that his time had not yet come; but she, convinced like most mothers that she knew what was best for her child, insisted on having her way and asked that the jugs be brought to Jesus.

There are only two places in the Gospels where Jesus lost an argument, and in both cases it was to a woman. This is the first instance. Judging by his amazing feat of changing sixty gallons of water into the best wine, it was obvious that his time had indeed come, in spite of Jesus' contention otherwise. Mary appeared to know what he needed and was right to ignore his argument.

It appeared Jesus was right in following Mary's lead and doing as she asked. It was because of this act, the Scriptures say, that the disciples believed in his divinity. In the Gospel of John, the writer presents seven signs that rewrite the creation motif with Jesus, the incarnation of God, at its center. The story of changing the water to wine is the first sign, and Mary is at the center of it.

Part of the reason for our devotion to Mary lies in her faithfulness to God's will in the face of opposition. If we were more relentless in our desire to live faithfully, maybe the question of how to balance our lives would recede somewhat in our minds. Saints throughout history have shown devotion to Mary and have committed themselves to that devotion. Let's look at two of those saints briefly and then hear the story of one contemporary mother.

Francis de Sales was born in 1567 in France. He was ordained in 1593 and became Bishop of Geneva. He was a great teacher of Christian spirituality and spoke eloquently about devotion to God. He wrote that our aim in faith should be true devotion.

> As a Christian, you know how acceptable this is to God. Small errors, at the beginning, can become almost irreparable. First, then, you must find out the nature of this virtue, because there is only one true devotion and the others are false and empty. . . . Living devotion presupposes the love of God; indeed, it is itself a true love of him in the highest form. Divine love, enlightening our soul and making us pleasing to God, is called grace. Giving us power to do good, it is called charity. When it reaches the point of perfection [as it did for Mary], . . . it is called devotion.

He wrote later:

> Charity and devotion differ no more than the flame from the fire. Charity is a spiritual fire, which breaks out into flame and is then called devotion. Devotion

simply adds a flame to the fire of charity which makes it ready, active, and diligent not only in keeping God's commandments but also in carrying out the heavenly counsels and inspirations.

(The Joy of the Saints: Spiritual Readings Throughout the Year, Darton, Longman and Todd, 1988; pages 34–35)

Julian of Norwich was born some three hundred years before Francis de Sales but shared his love for devoted prayer and union with God. Julian was a mystic who received a series of visions from God when she was seriously ill at the age of thirty. She recorded these visions in *The Revelations of Divine Love,* regarded as a spiritual classic. In one vision she recalled being visited by the virgin Mary.

In my mind I saw her as if she breathed—a simple, humble girl, not much more than a child; the age she was when she conceived. God showed me, too, in part, the wisdom and truth of her soul, so that I understood the reverence she felt before God her maker and how she marveled that he would be born of her—a simple soul that he himself had made. It was this wisdom and this truth in her that showed her the greatness of her maker and the smallness of herself whom he had made. And it was this that made her say so humbly to Gabriel, "Behold God's handmaid." By this I know surely that she is higher in worth and grace than anyone that God has made. For no one that is made is above her, except the blessed humanity of Christ.

There are also women today following the devoted path of Mary. Just this week I received an e-mail from a young mother whose six-month-old son, Charlie, was diagnosed with brain cancer. From the moment of his diagnosis, his mother became as vigilant and faithful as Mary. She began a circle of prayer for Charlie and kept enlisting anyone within earshot to join "Charlie's Angels." She took him to the best hospitals in the country for treatment and never stopped giving God thanks for the gift of motherhood and Charlie. Charlie has outlived the survival statistics and is currently nine months out of treatment. Charlie, his mother, grandmother, and father just returned from a trip to Lourdes, France, to bathe in the holy waters dedicated to the virgin Mary. Here is her account of their time there:

Last winter, my sister-in-law's mother gave us a bottle of Holy Water from Lourdes, France. Each night David (Charlie's father) puts a drop of the water in the sign of a cross on Charlie's forehead and then we say a prayer. We made a pact that when Charlie was well enough, we would make a pilgrimage to Lourdes and bathe Charlie in the water. Lourdes is a place that makes you feel that the very air you breathe is Holy. We were bathed and prayed over together in these beautiful baths and it was a powerfully emotional experience. The water was "take-your-breath-away cold" but when you stepped out you were warm and peaceful. We each were assigned our own handmaiden who undressed us and guided us into the ritual of the baths. (Charlie had five women!) It was such a beautiful, quiet experience to be surrounded by these French women praying in French so devoutly for us in the name of the Virgin Mary. I think to be surrounded by people that are so faithful, believe so strongly in the possibilities of God's love, presence, and miracles, it allows you a glimpse into God's heart. We felt such a sense of peace and hope in the world.

Farrell Mason
(November 22, 2003)

Reflecting and Recording

How do you see your devotion to God lived out in duty to those you love?

If you listed things you were devoted to on one side of a page and things that you felt a duty toward on the other side, would the lists be different? How would they be related?

Prayer

Almighty God, who has fashioned us to carry out your purpose, that your son might be manifested in each one of us, grant us all, now and forever, to listen to your voice and yield ourselves to your will, that we may be conformed to your image. Amen.

DAY FIVE: MARY AT THE CROSS—GOD'S LOVE WILL ENDURE

John 19:25-28

Meanwhile, standing near the cross of Jesus were his mother,
and his mother's sister, Mary the wife of Clopas, and Mary Magdalene. When
Jesus saw his mother and the disciple whom he loved
standing beside her, he said to his mother, "Woman, here is your son."
Then he said to the disciple, "Here is your mother."
And from that hour the disciple took her into his own home.

Mary's actions throughout her life demonstrated how devoted she was to her family and to God. Though she is not mentioned again in the Gospel of John until the scene at the foot of the cross, we can imagine, because of Jesus' words to her at the end, that she has been with him throughout his ministry. She has had a quiet strength and endured a great deal of pain while watching her son be taken and crucified for his faith.

The scene at the cross is filled with symbolism and beauty. As the devotion of Mary to Jesus is transferred quietly to his beloved disciple, we witness that above all else Jesus wishes his ministry to continue. The scene is filled with tenderness and heartbreaking forgiveness. Mary's presence means that she forgives her son's willingness to give up his life for God. His death was surely the most painful thing he could ask his mother to endure. It is this scene that ennobles Mary as a saint. That she bore God's Son is a wonder; that she stayed with him throughout his ministry is loyalty; but to risk her own life and watch the death of her son is grace personified.

A drunk driver killed my father when I was five, and I remember my grandfather saying he would never get over it. He said that to bury your own child is so unnatural and painful that all you can do is pray. Throughout my ministry I have witnessed women grieving the loss of their sons on just four occasions. Each incident stands out in my mind, because the mothers seemed to be standing on a holy ground that no one can imagine. If it is our brokenness that connects us to the holy, these women are held in the bosom of God. It is the deaths of those we love, as well as their births, that fire our hearts and either shut us down or make us more faithful.

If we are going to try honestly to offer our hearts and minds to God, we have to be willing to endure the pain of loving. I believe that, through God's mercy, it is the very things we think will break us that can in fact become the foundation of our faith. They are the places of compassion in which we learn to hear the cry of the world. The death of my father was the beginning of my journey with God. In his death I learned about forgiveness, the love of community, and the hope of resurrection.

A few weeks ago, Clemmie, a graduate of Magdalene, lost her son. His name was Rodriguez, and he was shot during the night on a street corner. He and his mom had been in recovery together for a couple of years. When she graduated from Magdalene, she started her own ministry, reaching out to addicts suffering on the streets. Clemmie is a powerful preacher and has been a great witness to the power of recovery. So it was especially horrible that drugs and violence took her only son still in his twenties.

After we buried him, Clemmie and I went back to her office to talk. As we spoke about the night he died and the young man who shot him, she said, "I wish I could talk to the boy before they take him to prison, and tell him that I forgive him." All I could do was weep. I had longed to hear those powerful words of forgiveness as long as I had known to listen for them. Clemmie seemed just like Mary at the foot of the cross, forgiving and loving, even in the most painful experience of her life. I told her that if she was going to remain faithful and committed, I would, too. I promised never to quit trying to make our community safer for our children and for loving our neighbors. Clemmie is a powerful example for us all. She is living proof that no matter what happens in our lives, it is not a test of our faith but a part of life that our faith can endure. Clemmie reminds us that the love and devotion of Mary are possible for all of us.

Part of what is so powerful about Mary is that she speaks to us with no words. It is simply her presence that demonstrates the truth we know in our hearts. There have been many women like Mary who have been silent witnesses to truth. One of the great examples of this quiet strength and devotion is the mother of the Civil Rights Movement, Rosa Parks. She was a witness to justice by sitting on a bus. It was such a clear and profound act that it helped launch the successful bus boycotts of the late 1950s in Alabama and other parts of the South, and it ushered in a new era for civil rights.

In her book *Quiet Strength* (Zondervan, 1994), Rosa Parks writes of the need to live out our faith with duty and devotion:

If you want to be respected for your actions, then your behavior must be above reproach. I learned from my grandmother and mother that one should always respect oneself and live right. This is how you gain the respect of others. If our lives demonstrate that we are peaceful, humble and trusted, this is recognized by others. If our lives demonstrate something else, that will be noticed too.

She adds:

Daily devotions played an important part in my childhood. Every day before supper, and before we went to services on Sundays, my grandmother would read the Bible to me, and my grandfather would pray. We even had devotions before going to pick cotton in the fields.

Parks goes on to write that she chooses never to become discouraged as long as people are still trying to make the world better, and that her faith has given her a quiet strength that comes from the Bible.

Reflecting and Recording

What gives you quiet strength in your day?

What has death taught you about your life?

In your desire to serve God first, what stands in your path?

Prayer

So draw our hearts to you, so guide our minds, so fill our imaginations, so control our wills, that we may be wholly yours. Amen.

(Book of Common Worship, 833)

DAY SIX: THE IMAGE OF THE SACRED HEART

John 3: 5-8

Very truly, I tell you, no one can enter the kingdom of God without being born of water and Spirit. What is born of the flesh is flesh, and what is born of the Spirit is spirit. Do not be astonished that I said to you, "You must be born from above." The wind blows where it chooses, and you hear the sound of it, but you do not know where it comes from or where it goes. So it is with everyone who is born of the Spirit.

Among the icons and images of Mary, there is one in which she is bearing her heart, and we can see flames surrounding it with a dove on top. The image shows that symbolically her heart, which is completely devoted to God, could not be broken, even in witnessing the death of her son, but instead blazed with the glory of passion. She has the laws written on her heart and bears that heart for the world. She can bear our pain and hear our cries, since she has suffered so great a loss for the sake of the Kingdom. This image of Mary reminds us of the cost of true devotion and the depth of real duty.

Clare, the woman who lived out the ideals of Francis of Assisi in great humility and love, wrote to one of her sisters, Agnes in Prague, that "if you suffer with Jesus, you shall reign with him as promised in 2 Timothy 2:12. And if you weep with him, you shall rejoice with him. And if you die with him on the cross of tribulation, you shall possess heavenly mansions in the splendor of the saints, and in the Book of Life, your name shall be called glorious among men." At the end of her life, Clare blessed her fellow sisters in the name of the Lord. She asked them always to be lovers of God and eager to observe what they have promised the Lord. Clare suffered as a result of her faith and, in being faithful and true in her devotion and duty, found her life ultimately full of blessedness and thankfulness.

This is also how it works for you and me. If we can endure, be sure in our faith, and always keep our hearts open to God, we will find that our lives have indeed been blessed. This does not mean that there won't be hardships, but that through them we will be graced with God's presence. The hardships, we discover, are not tests of our faith, but part of the journey of being alive and of having a sacred heart. As Jesus says to Nicodemus, we must be born of the Spirit to feel our hearts filled with God. If we can give our hearts and minds to God, surrendering ourselves, we will be graced with lives filled with love and mercy.

Reflecting and Recording

When you pray, do you feel a burning desire in your heart?

Can you name a woman who, to you, represents the sacred heart?

Prayer

Teach me, Lord, how to desire nothing more than to love you. Teach me, Lord, how to settle for nothing less than to be completely devoted to you. Teach me, Lord, how to make my heart yours. Amen.

DAY SEVEN: PREPARING FOR GROUP DISCUSSION

What are your thoughts about the relationship between birth and death? How do birth and death help you form your faith? What are some of the earliest and most formative ideas about faith that you maintain today? Why?

For years I longed to pray
Unaware the longing was the prayer.
So I offered my longing to God
Like aged port wine
And asked, "Will you drink from this cup?"
God returned my cup to me
Filled with fragrant blossoms grown
From the longing planted in me
Before I knew its name.
And I gave thanks that
The prayer I prayed was God's prayer for me.

Week Four:
The Canaanite Woman

Mark 3:1-6

Again he entered the synagogue, and a man was there who had a withered hand.
They watched him to see whether he would cure him on the sabbath,
so that they might accuse him. And he said to the man who had the withered hand,
"Come forward." Then he said to them, "Is it lawful to do good or to do harm
on the sabbath, to save life or to kill?" But they were silent.
He looked around at them with anger; he was grieved
at their hardness of heart and said to the man, "Stretch out your hand."
He stretched it out, and his hand was restored. The Pharisees went out
and immediately conspired with the Herodians against him, how to destroy him.

This week we will talk about what it means to be foreign and about the gifts we can discover in learning about our own otherness. This is a time to reflect upon the parts of our lives in which we judge ourselves or others as "unworthy," the places that keep our hearts and minds from union with God.

One of the themes for this week is religious tolerance. Religious tolerance involves demonstrating love for people of other faiths and tolerance for people who understand their Christian faith differently from us. It is important, because as long as we use Scripture to keep ourselves apart from others or to judge others, Scripture is used not for mercy but for might. I have often thought that whenever I see someone with a Bible in her hand, there is a good chance that she has something up her sleeve. This may seem strange coming from the author of a book dedicated to the study of Scripture, but too often people pull out quotes from the Bible to further their own prejudices and agendas. I have stopped engaging in arguments with people who quote one-line verses to back up their arguments. The truth is that you can find a Scripture to back up just about any argument, including the need for women to be silent and the practice of slavery.

When I am studying Scripture and learning about texts, I try to remember that the overall theme that Jesus preached was feeding the hungry, caring for the poor, and believing in him. When Jesus preaches, it is to me and you—to keep us mindful of our need for mercy and the fact that none of us will get what we deserve, thank God! Never did Jesus preach about memorizing the texts; in fact, in today's text Jesus was frustrated by the laws and people's desire to use them to prevent a man from receiving healing. This text is a great illustration of how religious laws can be used to hurt others rather than heal them.

Another thing we must remember is that the church created the Bible; the Bible didn't create the church. As far as we know, Jesus never wrote down his teachings. He spent his three years of active ministry healing and teaching, and it wasn't until at least A.D. 60 that we find the first of the written traditions that form the four Gospels. Each of these traditions is different and offers a different perspective on who Jesus is and what happened to him during his life and death. We even have differing accounts of how he was resurrected.

This fact is important to remember, especially as we try to allow what we read and study to inspire our daily actions. Our actions need to reflect an understanding of the overall theme in the Gospels—that we are not here to judge others but to walk in gratitude and love, just as God has shown us love again and again. As we pray alone, let us remember the image of Jesus walking into the synagogue and seeing the leaders in pious prayer as a man sits nearby, suffering. When Jesus healed the man, the leaders, instead of bursting with joy, rebuked him for breaking the law; and they conspired to destroy him. As we enter this day and walk in prayer so that our hearts and minds can love God, we need to pray to be open in our faith to others.

Reflecting and Recording

Have you ever felt that you have missed an opportunity to see God in others because you thought their beliefs were wrong?

What does it mean to think that others are "wrong" in their beliefs?

How do we teach one another lovingly if we feel that beliefs are false or wrong?

Prayer

O Lord, when we enter our house of prayer, let us have thanksgiving in our hearts. When we leave the house today, we promise to obey your commandments, not just with our lips but also in our lives, loving one another as you have loved us. Amen.

DAY TWO: A GREAT AND TENACIOUS FAITH

Matthew 15:21-28

Jesus left that place and went away to the district of Tyre and Sidon.
Just then a Canaanite woman from that region came out and started shouting,
"Have mercy on me, Lord, Son of David; my daughter is tormented by a demon."
But he did not answer her at all. And his disciples came and urged him, saying,
"Send her away, for she keeps shouting after us."
He answered, "I was sent only to the lost sheep of the house of Israel."
But she came and knelt before him, saying, "Lord, help me."
He answered, "It is not fair to take the children's food and throw it to the dogs."
She said, "Yes, Lord, yet even the dogs eat the crumbs that fall
from their masters' table." Then Jesus answered her, "Woman, great is your faith!
Let it be done for you as you wish." And her daughter was healed instantly.

In the Gospel of Matthew, Jesus traveled to the outskirts of Israel to the districts of Tyre and Sidon, and he encountered a woman from that region who engaged him in the second argument he lost in the New Testament. (The first was with Mary at the wedding in Cana.) One of the most interesting things that the woman in this Gospel demonstrated is that the message of Jesus is universal, and that the covenant is for all the children of God. It is this woman who won in her banter with Jesus; and because she did, the healing ministry of Jesus extended beyond national and religious borders.

In the story, the woman came and knelt before him, lost in her worry over her daughter. "Lord, help me!" she shouted. After an exchange of puzzling words that we will examine later in the week, Jesus finally answered, "Woman, great is your faith!"

The first thing that is curious about this passage is that it appears to be out of character for the Canaanite woman. As a Canaanite, she would not be engaging the group from the House of Israel, those who are the focus of much of Matthew's Gospel. She is a Gentile and is supposed to be unworthy and unclean. However, Matthew's Gospel gives special status to those who are seen as unworthy, such as foreigners, prostitutes, and tax collectors. Matthew's interest lies in restoring dignity and wholeness to all those who have been left out and marginalized.

This exchange also seems out of character for Jesus, who has spent the first fifteen chapters of Matthew wandering around Judea healing lepers and preaching the message not to judge others. While his encounter with the Canaanite woman is a source of much speculation, the most remarkable part of this brief and bewildering exchange is Jesus' conclusion that she has great faith. Somehow in the exchange and in the process of stepping out of their usual roles, he sees her faith and commends it.

If you scan the entire Bible looking for the expression *great faith,* you will find it in only two places, both in the New Testament. One concerns the Canaanite woman of our Gospel text; the other concerns the centurion in Capernaum whose servant was deathly ill. In both cases the individuals were Gentile (non-Jewish), and Jesus was the one to praise their faith. Neither of these two people claimed any special privilege, in fact, quite the contrary. The centurion did not consider himself even worthy to invite Jesus into his home; and the woman was satisfied to be considered a "dog," worthy only of the crumbs or morsels that fell from the table.

But the Canaanite woman, a Gentile, believed in Christ. In this passage she is the one restoring the covenant of God with God's people, and she is not relying on a birthright or ancestry for her salvation. Christ was the object of her faith and as a result Jesus described her faith as great, an accolade that was never applied to any other believer except the centurion—not even to the prophets or apostles.

What was it, then, that Jesus commended in her? He said, "Woman, great is your faith." Did she have faith in Jesus as a miracle worker for her daughter? Was it faith in herself that no matter what, for the sake of her daughter, she would prevail? Was it faith in a God who would ultimately choose for her, a woman utterly devoted to her daughter? When a person asks for mercy, such an attitude completely rules out any thought of merit, for mercy is the forbearance of punishment rightly deserved. No, the Canaanite woman did not rely upon herself at all. She even accepted the apparently insulting characterization of herself as a Gentile "dog" without complaining; rather, she insisted that even an unworthy dog (such as she) could at least receive the crumbs that are otherwise discarded.

Such humility and persistence! It is as if she said to Jesus, "I know I deserve nothing from you at all. Yet, you promised to be merciful and hear my prayers on behalf of my poor daughter. I'm holding you to your promise! I will not stop pleading with you until you answer my prayer. I believe you when you promise something, and I trust that you will fulfill your promise." That is faith in God—knowledge of the word and promises of God, and the trust that what God says is true and applies to us.

True faith, the kind that Jesus commends, knows only humility, for "I am sinful and unclean." It knows Jesus Christ as the Son of David, which is a title for the Messiah. It knows Jesus Christ as the God of creation, redemption, and sanctification. It knows Jesus Christ as the Savior, not only of the "lost sheep" whom he has come to save but also of all the nations of the world. It knows that only the blood of Christ has the power to wash away all our sins. It trusts in all this knowledge and in nothing else.

Christ heard and granted the request of the Canaanite woman for one reason—her faith. He praised her for her great faith, because she so firmly believed in God's promises. Though she was not a Jew, she persisted in her prayer and would not give up. Christ commends us to pray with complete confidence that he hears and answers us in ways that are always for our good.

Never give up praying for others whose need is just as great as ours, who need the mercy of God just as do we, and for whom God willingly will grant mercy for the sake of Christ, our Savior.

Reflecting and Recording

Beyond your duty and devotion there is a place where the real you is seen by God. How is that place affected by or a part of your faith?

Prayer

Give us the grace today that the words we read with our eyes be grafted into our hearts, that they may bring forth in us the fruit of faithful living, so that all we do and say will be a great witness to your loving mercy. Amen.

DAY THREE: FEELING LIKE A FOREIGNER

Mark 7:25-30

A woman whose little daughter had an unclean spirit immediately heard
about him, and she came and bowed down at his feet.
Now the woman was a Gentile, of Syrophoenician origin. She begged him
to cast the demon out of her daughter. He said to her, "Let the children be fed first,
for it is not fair to take the children's food and throw it to the dogs."
But she answered him, "Sir, even the dogs under the table
eat the children's crumbs." Then he said to her,
"For saying that, you may go—the demon has left your daughter."

In this version of Jesus' encounter with the woman in the Gospel of Mark, she is Syrophoenician, not Canaanite; and Jesus doesn't praise her great faith but instead tells her that because of her words, her daughter will be made well. As in the Matthew passage, she is a foreigner, and she is treated as such by Jesus.

Being a foreigner in first-century Palestine must have been incredibly difficult; and there is something about being a woman that helps us relate to that foreign feeling. I have seen it many times in my work as director of Magdalene. Whenever I speak to a group of women (whether a church or business group) about the women of Magdalene as being abused early in their lives and being alienated from their communities, heads always nod in sympathy. We can all appreciate and relate to events that make us question how it is that we belong, and who it is that we belong to.

Sometimes, as we are trying to live our lives faithfully, we can feel like foreigners in our homes, churches, and families. We feel out of step and sense that people can see that we feel less than worthy. That is why the Syrophoenician or Canaanite woman is a great figure to study as we talk about duty and devotion. We are never going to get the balance exactly right, or even know what exactly "right" looks like. We can fret, worry, and stay hidden from Christ; or we can stand before him as the Canaanite woman and say, "Here I am, and this is my prayer." Often I have felt a great affinity with the Canaanite woman.

There is a shoe store that has been around for thirty years on the side of the main entrance of a local mall. It is completely glassed in and filled with single shoes displayed along glass counters on clear shoe horns. I have never been inside, although the other day as I walked past, it occurred to me for the first time that I could go inside. Unconsciously since childhood, entering this store has not been an option for me. I don't know if it's because it looks expensive, or because my mom's idea of new shoes was a pair of old canvas tennis shoes with a new application of white shoe polish. Shoes were one of the first symbols I remember of priesthood. I was ordained in clogs, as I knelt in the middle of a huddle of priests laying hands on me. When I opened my eyes for a moment, I noticed that I was surrounded by black shoes, mostly tasseled. I thought, "It is going to be hard to wear my shoes in this job."

Something about shoes still eludes me. I went to talk to the bishop about our desire to rebuild our chapel sanctuary. I thought I should look nice, so I went across the street to my neighbor, "the Imelda Marcos of Nashville," and borrowed a bone sandal with a modest heel. I heard later that there was a conversation after the meeting about my clothing ensemble; the sentiment expressed was that the way I was dressed hadn't helped my cause. Sometimes as a woman one can't win. Judged by our shoes, we regularly judge others by their shoes and clothing. Women are frequently left out because of what we say, what we don't say, or for being too forward, too crass, too sexy, or too uptight; we end up feeling alien in our own country.

The homecoming queen of feeling alien, though, has got to be the Canaanite woman in the Gospel of Matthew. There she is in the story, alone and poor and dismissed by the disciples for being both. But the intimacy she achieves with Jesus is a powerful sign that we should stand in our own shoes and move beyond all the political, social, and religious barriers. She is funny, uncovering truth in witty repartee while standing toe to toe with the Lord. She is a heroine who celebrates the freedom that our otherness gives us to speak the truth and plead our case.

The modern Canaanite woman doesn't go into glass rooms, even if there aren't any visible signs to stop her. She knows better. She knows the silence or dismissive comments that may greet her. She knows that the power is not in her hands, no matter how strong they are. When we, like the Canaanite woman, become desperate enough to move beyond the glass walls because of our greater need for truth, the promise is that we too will find freedom, health, and intimacy with our Lord. Out of her great courage, she encourages us to stand in our shoes. Out of her spirit we are inspired to believe that when we are outside the inner sanctum, under the glass ceiling, or left to tie our own bootstraps, it is a gift.

She speaks to all of us in our otherness in this world. Although I do not know what it is like to be Iraqi, or African American, or gay, or blind, or have a criminal record, I do know a little about my otherness; and the Canaanite woman makes me thankful for it. The otherness is the place through which we find our way to God. In filling our shoes we make strange tracks, but that is the path we walk to holiness. In that walk, a new gospel is written, love is discovered, and lives are saved. It is from this path that we learn that love can be radical and can save us. The Canaanite woman is fortunate to know her otherness well enough so that when she encounters the Lord, she falls at his feet, shouting for mercy. She is blessed because she knows that her hope lies not in her heritage, but in God's loving mercy.

Really she should be proud of what she did. Repeatedly in the Gospels, the disciples miss Jesus' vision and purpose in healing those around him. A friend of mine calls the disciples in the Gospel of Mark "the original Marx brothers." They are always perplexed by Jesus' actions, from giving food to the five thousand, to calming the storm, to admonishing them for wanting to sit at the right and left hand of God in the Kingdom. You and I are much more like them than we care to admit. But the Canaanite woman gets it right and in doing so reminds us that even the crumbs of Jesus thrown to the dogs are more than we could have imagined. Those crumbs were enough to heal the woman's daughter.

Reflecting and Recording

Do you sometimes feel like a foreigner? If so, when do you get those feelings, and why?

Are there places, such as the shoe store for me, that you have never wanted to enter?

Who are people you have treated as foreigners?

Prayer

We thank you for calling us out of sameness and dullness of mind to remember who we are and whose we are. Thank you for making us in your image, unique in all the world. Give us the strength to stand in our own shoes and to walk the path you have set before us. Amen.

DAY FOUR: DOG DAYS

It is startling to hear these words come from Jesus' lips: "It is not fair to take the children's food and throw it to the dogs." Is this Jesus on a bad day, or was he really just trying to insult a desperate woman needing his help? It is a troubling example of a passage we tend to gloss over so that we can get to the beautiful and loving passages. Why did Jesus seem to insult the Canaanite woman by referring to her as a dog?

To a Jew, a dog is an unclean animal (that is, ceremonially unclean). If a Jew called a Samaritan, Roman, or Canaanite person a dog, it meant that the person was unworthy of God's kingdom and was worthy only to receive the garbage that the Jews left to rot and spoil. Of course, this was an attitude that they usually kept to themselves, particularly in the presence of Roman soldiers. Nevertheless, the Jews looked down on their Gentile neighbors, considering them unworthy of God and of receiving God's blessings.

When Jesus referred to the Canaanite woman as a dog, she responded in a manner that was smart, unflinching, and disarming. The woman certainly lacked no awareness of the power and significance of Jesus; indeed, she seemed to know this better than most. This awareness, though, did not inhibit her from standing her ground before him. It was indeed holy ground, and she knew that she must remain there, however dangerous and strange it might seem. Her faith can help us to shape our own faithful responses to God. Like her, we can fall on our knees for mercy and then stand on the ground we know to be holy, speaking our hearts to God for healing and mercy.

The closest I ever came to meeting the Canaanite woman was Peggy Sue, a prisoner who was dying in state custody at a local hospital. I saw a high school picture of Peggy Sue, and she had been beautiful. She had become a baker, but then she had ended up living on the streets and in jails. After three years of this lifestyle, she had contracted AIDS and syphilis. When we met, she weighed about eighty-five pounds and could no longer eat. She asked for God's mercy every time I saw her; and since she knew the Scriptures better than I did, we would sit and talk about different passages. She looked as if she were carrying the sins of the world on her broken body: all the degrading ways we treat one another, the pain of loneliness, and the cost of the whole world's using sex like a drug. She looked as if, like the Canaanite woman, she had been eating table scraps for a long time.

Near the end, it was painful to go and see her. The ravages of the diseases on her body caused me usually to fall into silent prayer. In one of those prayers, I saw her in a vision lying in repose in the lap of Jesus. She looked completely peaceful and beautiful again. I could see Jesus, head down, crying—not for her, but for all of us who, through complacency, ignorance, or self-interest, have allowed this world to be in such pain.

For Peggy Sue's funeral, the state gave us a cardboard box with her ashes in it and a room to use for a service. One of the seven women who came to the service picked up a rose on the way in and placed it by the cardboard box. I kept thinking that this was the worst it could ever be: a horrible life and death and now this empty funeral on top of it. Just as we began the first prayer, all of us in the circle started to cry. There was an overwhelming sense of God's mercy and presence filling the room. It occurred to me that when there is nothing else filling the space, God's grace does.

Whatever life brings, I will take it, because even at its absolute worst there is always grace. Since that service I have never doubted the passage about the Canaanite woman. It makes sense to me that God saw her great faith and that Jesus felt a closeness and a kinship with her that allowed them to banter and care for each other.

Reflecting and Recording

Have you ever been surprised by grace? Describe the situation and how you responded.

Prayer

O God, the source of peace and grace in a world of turmoil, the fountain of meaning in a world that sometimes seems cruel and confusing: Grant us the assurance of your grace as we seek to serve you and to love you all the days of our lives. Thank you for your presence in our lives every day that allows us to praise you with our words and in our deeds. Amen.

DAY FIVE: THE NEED FOR SOCIAL JUSTICE
IN DUTY AND DEVOTION

Matthew 12:1-2, 6-7

At that time Jesus went through the cornfields on the sabbath;
his disciples were hungry, and they began to pluck heads of grain and to eat.
When the Pharisees saw it, they said to him, "Look, your disciples are doing
what is not lawful to do on the sabbath.". . .
[Jesus said], "I tell you, something greater than the temple is here.
But if you had known what this means, 'I desire mercy and not sacrifice,' you
would not have condemned the guiltless. For the Son of Man is lord of the sabbath."

This passage appears about three chapters before Jesus met the Canaanite woman. First, Jesus and the disciples plucked the grains in the field; next, they walked into the synagogue and Jesus healed the man with the withered hand (Mark 3:1-6); and then, he preached in parables about the kingdom of heaven. He then fed the five thousand, walked on the water, healed some very sick people, and encountered the Canaanite woman. In this sequence of events, Jesus continually distanced himself from the religious authority and made it clear that the Kingdom he was talking about was vastly different from any kingdom we have known. Everything he did and said in these critical chapters reflected his concern for people rather than laws, and for justice rather than the status quo.

Many times this part of the message is overlooked when we are doing an inventory of our faith. It can be difficult to see where we are focusing on laws for our convenience and because of our privilege, and neglecting the gospel.

95

It is easy to pass over the voice of the nameless Canaanite woman; we won't see her again, and she doesn't have any power over us. It's doubly ironic if we neglect the Canaanite woman because she is unfamiliar to us and we see her as really weird or different. Her marginal position is, in fact, the point of the story.

When we read the Bible, we often forget to look at the perspective of the Canaanites, the Gentiles, or whoever the outsiders are. How does Jesus look from the perspective of the Canaanite woman? He must seem safe and powerful, because she was free enough to shout and speak plainly with him. She shouted and screamed and made a bother of herself because her heart had been wrenched by the desperate illness of her daughter. Today, many other mothers find themselves crying out to God for their children. From the very deepest despair comes naked anguish pouring out in grief or pleading. For many, the first act of faith is an act like this, a call for rescue or maybe just a cry that doesn't know a purpose. At times, neat and tidy religion doesn't quite know what to do with despair like this. The too-hasty search for answers or sheer embarrassment in the face of undignified need can prevent us from doing what the psalmist does so naturally—lament. A howl that can seem ugly and can disturb us may be a truer picture of faith than a religion of cold duty and soulless propriety. Our self-contained contentedness may not allow much room for us to receive the light of God.

It is our willingness to hear those hard cries from others, and from ourselves, that keeps us honest in our relationship to God. The cries are not pleasant, but they express the reality of life, especially if you think about the circumstances in our world. There are thousands and thousands of abandoned children in southern Africa whose parents have died of AIDS. Tens of thousands die from natural disasters, leaving behind countless grieving families. Close to two million people are in our jail systems, with over eight percent of them there because of drug-related problems. These people have grieving and worried families. It is our job, as we pray and work for the Kingdom that Jesus preaches about, to hear the cries of all the Canaanite women in our midst.

The woman, through her cry, offers us a gift: profound awareness of God's mercy. "Have mercy on me, Lord, Son of David," calls the woman, thus uttering the distinctive Christian prayer: Have mercy, *Kyrie eleison.* The Canaanite woman knows that God acts mercifully because God is mercy. Rejection and condemnation are not the essence of God, but mercy is; and the mercy of God is undiscriminating, profligate, and passionate. God is merciful to those we shun and pours love upon those we can't bear to look at. If we truly grasped that truth, our world might be very different.

It is important that Matthew chooses to label this woman a Canaanite. It is an odd and archaic description, and he uses it to emphasize the extent to which she would be hated by the disciples as a pagan, an idolater, perhaps even a member of a privileged foreign element who thrived at the expense of the local population. The woman is the victim of deep prejudice, so her faith has the additional power of having overcome huge obstacles. Her presence in this story comes as a challenge to us. How many times have we heard or, indeed, uttered a sentence that begins: "Now, I'm not a racist, but . . ."? We erect barriers that prevent us from recognizing fellow human beings by making all manner of assumptions about them. This recognition, when it occurs, links us to our sense of God's mercy for all. As soon as we insert that prejudging "but" into our awareness of others, we limit the extent to which we can see them as beloved of God. The Canaanite woman dares us to see beyond our "buts."

Reflecting and Recording

Can you remember a time when you cried out to God?

How did that affect your relationship with God?

Prayer

Dear Lord, who calls not the well but the sick to repentance, anoint us to be agents of your healing ministry. Send us out this day to hear the cries of those who suffer, so that we can loosen the bonds of wickedness, free the oppressed, feed the hungry, and clothe the naked. All this we do in gratitude for the healing we have found in our own lives. Amen.

DAY SIX: PIECING IT ALL TOGETHER

The Scripture from Matthew tells us that one day the Lord was in the land of Canaan, to the north of Israel. This is significant. There had long been animosity between the Jews and the Canaanites since the time of Abraham. Therefore, for the Lord to be in the land of Canaan was a bold statement. While he was there, a Canaanite woman came begging him to heal her daughter, who was possessed by a demon. The woman was desperate to have her daughter become sound again. She was even willing to go to a Jew and plead with him to heal her daughter. The Canaanite woman was not too proud to submit herself to the Lord for the sake of her daughter, especially when she realized that her child could only be healed by him.

We also must be willing to go to the Lord without pride and be willing to submit ourselves to him. We must acknowledge and confess that we are incapable of overcoming our difficulties, especially our spiritual ones, through our own power. Instead we are entirely dependent on the Lord's power to heal us. Like the Canaanite woman who came to Jesus fully realizing that she could not remove her daughter's demon with her own strength, so too must we approach the Lord fully realizing that our deliverance can only come from him.

If we come before the Lord with conditions, saying what we can and cannot do, we are approaching from a position of pride. If, however, we approach the Lord with the willingness to submit ourselves to anything he would have us do, no matter what, then we acknowledge his power and our dependence on him. This is one of the lessons that twelve-step program participants learn and use in their healing process. The willingness to submit to a higher power, to try to live another way, is the first step people must take when they want to be made well.

During times of trouble, quite often we feel the same desperation and frustration the Canaanite woman did. Sometimes when we are struggling, the Lord does not seem to respond. And when there is an answer, it often is not what we want to hear. The Lord seems to be telling us what he told the Canaanite woman: "I was sent only to the lost sheep of the house of Israel" (Matthew 15:24). In the face of that resistance, she did not give up but continued to ask the Lord to heal her daughter. When the Lord told her that it is not good to give bread to the dogs, she responded by saying, "Yes, Lord, yet even the dogs eat the crumbs that fall from their master's table" (Matthew 15:26). She was willing to call herself a dog to help her child. In spite of the rejection she had endured to that point, she still believed in the Lord's compassion and did not let pride prevent her daughter's healing.

The Canaanite woman's perseverance offers us a great lesson. We must continually strive to do the best we can to live according to the teachings of the Lord. We must maintain faith in the Lord's mercy and love and know that he will never forsake us, no matter how desperate our situation. We also must be humble. Certainly the Canaanite woman could have turned away from the Lord when he ignored and insulted her. But because she loved her daughter more than herself, she was able to stand firm in spite of the harsh treatment. If we strive to love the Lord and others before ourselves, we will be able to remain true to this dedication in spite of the trials we endure; and, like the Canaanite woman, we will eventually have our needs met.

The great lesson this woman teaches us this week is that we are no more and no less than the children of God. We are all made worthy to stand before God, by the same grace that healed the woman's daughter and made Jesus see her "great faith." Whenever we are trying to discern how to live dutifully and devotedly, let us keep the Canaanite woman close to our hearts so that we never become too proud or lose our way. She helps us achieve the humility we need and the intimacy we desire with our Lord. Thanks be to God for the Canaanite woman.

Reflecting and Recording

Can you think of something that you would like to do differently in your life of prayer and service in light of the lessons that the Canaanite woman has taught us this week?

Prayer

O Holy God, thank you for the times of trial as well as the times of joy. Thank you for reminding us again through the witness of the Canaanite woman that we never have to live alienated from ourselves or one another. Have compassion on us always; send your spirit to heal us and to prepare us for the work you have planned for us. Your praise shall always be on our lips, and we shall exalt your name. Amen.

DAY SEVEN: PREPARING FOR GROUP DISCUSSION

In some ways this has been the most challenging week for me to write. In what ways has it been challenging to you?

I carry on my journey
A bag, freshly painted
With blooming lily fields
Set against a sunny sky.

Inside are the secret silver coins
I have held so dear.
I wish rust would rid me of them
Or a thief would break in.

It's not enough for me to empty it on the altar
And ask for forgiveness from God
Hoping that a miracle
Will take them from my hands.

I want to place each coin in your lap
That was the altar of my youth
And tell the tender stories of their gathering
As you hold them up as a sacred offering.

Then we could start a fire and burn the bag
And laugh and dance,
Unburdened by useless treasures
Once held more worthy than gold.

Week Five:
Mary Magdalene

DAY ONE: THE MYSTERIOUS DISCIPLE

Luke 7:36-39, 48–8:3

One of the Pharisees asked Jesus to eat with him,
and he went into the Pharisee's house and took his place at the table.
And a woman in the city, who was a sinner, having learned that he was eating
in the Pharisee's house, brought an alabaster jar of ointment.
She stood behind him at his feet, weeping, and began to bathe his feet
with her tears and to dry them with her hair. Then she continued kissing his feet
and anointing them with the ointment. Now when the Pharisee
who had invited him saw it, he said to himself,
"If this man were a prophet, he would have known who
and what kind of woman this is who is touching him—that she is a sinner."
. . . Then he said to her, "Your sins are forgiven."
But those who were at the table with him began to say among themselves,
"Who is this who even forgives sins?" And he said to the woman,
"Your faith has saved you; go in peace." Soon afterwards he went on through cities
and villages, proclaiming and bringing the good news of the kingdom of God.
The twelve were with him, as well as some women who had been cured
of evil spirits and infirmities: Mary, called Magdalene, from whom seven demons
had gone out, and Joanna the wife of Herod's steward, Chuza, and Susanna,
and many others, who provided for them out of their resources.

There is not a female character in the New Testament more fascinating and more misunderstood than Mary Magdalene. From the ideas presented in the best-selling novel *The DaVinci Code* to the old stereotypes of what constitutes a sinful woman, we make her into what we need her to be. Magdalene's introduction in the Gospels is surrounded by mystery. She emerges immediately after the scene of the sinful woman washing Jesus' feet but is never identified in the text as being that woman. She plays an important role in the Gospels, though, and any study of duty and devotion must focus on her role and what she has to say to us. Indeed, in the Eastern Church Magdalene has been regarded as the equal of an apostle. Early medieval traditions refer to Magdalene as the "Apostle of the Apostles."

Magdalene has played a key role in my own priestly formation. The program I founded is named after her, because I believe she embodies more than anyone else in the New Testament the power of grace and the intimacy of God's love for us. I see her as a grateful leader who stood with the disciples and held her own. It's fascinating to listen to what people, from feminists to conservative theologians, have to say about Magdalene. Whether she is defined as the first preacher, the thirteenth disciple, or a prostitute, the fact is that we don't know a lot about her or, for that matter, any other woman in the New Testament.

I have spent a great deal of time thinking about Magdalene and her witness and explaining why I would use her name for a program that rehabilitates prostitutes. Whether she was a prostitute or not doesn't really matter to me. Biblical scholars, I think, try and make that distinction mean more than it does. After working with women from the streets for the last decade, I have learned that there is really not so much difference between a priest and a prostitute. I remember sitting in a basilica in Minnesota and noticing that the wall to my left was lined with confession booths. The booths were ornately decorated and carved with saints. The one that I was sitting closest to bore the image of Mary Magdalene, her raised hand offering either absolution or welcome, I couldn't tell. I sat there imagining the lines of people over the last 150 years who must have walked into that house and confessed sins both great and small. If those booths could talk, they would simply tell the tale of the human condition, that we all have sinned and are all worthy of redemption.

What matters to God is that we stand in grace and give thanks and follow God's calling. That is what Magdalene did, and she did it in a circle that mostly consisted of men. She provided for the disciples and Jesus out of her own resources. Her presence at both the cross and the tomb points to her preeminence as a disciple. She is named fourteen times, more than any other woman in the Gospels except for Mary, Jesus' mother. From those references we can draw a sketchy profile of her life. We know that she was faithful, loyal, intimate with Jesus, and part of the inner circle of disciples. We know that whenever she is mentioned with a group of women, her name comes first, indicating that she was a leader among women. We know that she traveled with Jesus and witnessed the miracles.

Her name is interesting as well. The name Mary occurs fifty-one times in the New Testament and is taken from the Old Testament names of Miriam and Mara, which mean "bitter." The root of the name Mary is derived from the notion of trouble and sorrow. It was a common name during this time period, so this Mary was distinguished from all others by being called "The Magdalene." The name identifies her as being born in Magdala, a thriving city that lay on the northwest side of the Sea of Galilee, about three miles north of Tiberius. The city of Magdala was known for its textile factories and dye works. Scholars have speculated that perhaps Mary Magdalene was connected in some way with that industry, which might have enabled her to help support the ministry of Jesus, as she was known to have done.

We know from Luke's account that Magdalene had been "possessed by seven demons." Whether those were the demons of mental illness, sex, gluttony, pride, adultery, murder, or other sins, her community and family surely would have shunned her. Jesus, who could have passed her by or seen her as another leper, showed compassion and love; and he healed her. Her response was to follow Jesus, even after his arrest and death. Whatever happened in Mary Magdalene's past, her devotion to Christ was evident after her conversion. She came into the circle of believers, marked out from the rest by an exceptional experience of the Lord's healing power, and she followed Jesus to the end with untiring devotion and undaunted courage, even in the face of dangers that overcame the courage of the chosen Twelve.

In the Scriptures we learn that Christ's great love and compassion toward Magdalene completely changed her life and led her to become a faithful, sacrificial follower. So grateful was Magdalene for her deliverance that she practiced her faith by following Jesus and using her financial means to provide for the physical needs of Jesus and the disciples. Her gratitude and love manifested itself in her devotion to Christ.

Reflecting and Recording

What are your presumptions about Mary Magdalene?

Reflect on the times when you have felt closest to God.

Prayer

Almighty God, you have inspired us with the witness of Mary Magdalene. We pray for such courage and strength in our witness to your loving power. Amen.

DAY TWO: WOUNDED AND POWERFUL HEALERS

Luke 9:23-25

Then he said to them all, "If any want to become my followers,
let them deny themselves and take up their cross daily and follow me.
For those who want to save their life will lose it, and those who lose their life
for my sake will save it. What does it profit them
if they gain the whole world, but lose or forfeit themselves?"

Mary Magdalene joined Jesus in his ministry in the eighth chapter of Luke. Jesus then preached the parable of the sower, crossed the lake with his disciples, healed a demonic man and sent the evil spirits into a herd of swine, healed Jarius's daughter, healed a woman who had suffered from hemorrhages for twelve years, fed the five thousand, and took the inner circle up the mountain for the Transfiguration. All of this happened in just seventy-five verses. Then Jesus turned to his disciples and said that to save their lives they must pick up their crosses every day and follow him. For the women who had joined the disciples, it must have been a beautiful and poignant time, a time for them to give their lives to God in order to live well.

In my work with the women of Magdalene, I have learned that their voices are powerful because they are able to speak the truth, unafraid of what people will think. They have paid a high cost for that honesty, but it allows them to tell their stories with dignity and clarity. It is not in spite of their past but *because* of it that they are powerful ministers to the rest of us.

One thing that never works in the Gospels is for people to remain mired in the past. If we are blind, or have been bleeding for twenty years, or have seven demons in our lives, as long as we are faithful, Jesus can work through us to help heal others. Nothing in our past can stop that. The only thing that can stop us is when we allow ourselves to be defined by our past. Whatever Mary Magdalene's past, Jesus healed her and set her free.

One of the first things I remember learning in Pastoral Care 101 was that guilt needs to be forgiven, and shame needs to be accepted. This means that guilt and shame, two things that can hold us back from offering our hearts and minds to God, can be the means by which we learn the lessons of forgiveness and acceptance. There is nothing in our past that cannot be used for good. We can be like Mary and use the brokenness of our lives as a powerful foundation for a lifelong faith in Jesus. This is the first lesson that she teaches us: *Our past can be the means by which we find healing and truth in our lives.*

One of the traits that Mary Magdalene possessed, a trait that all of us could use on our faith journeys, is freedom. She was free to travel with the disciples, free to sit and eat with them, free to have conversations with Jesus, free to go wherever God's will called her. Once she had escaped her demons and completely surrendered her life to Jesus, she became a great minister. The same is true for each of us. Once we have completely surrendered ourselves to the will of God, we are completely free. This is the second lesson that Magdalene teaches us: *When we lose our life for the sake of the gospel, we gain it.*

Over and over again the Gospels teach us that what the world sees one way, we can see in a whole new light. These teachings can best be understood through the grace-filled paradoxes of Jesus. The places that the world sees as poor can be rich; the places where there is sadness can be joyful. So maybe it is possible that being something like a prostitute, which the world sees as the lowest place a woman could sink to, would be the highest place to learn the lesson of value and worth for a woman. This is not to say that we know for sure Magdalene was a prostitute; I'm just saying that it is possible that the woman given the highest esteem in the gospel would have that background. In every glimpse we have of Magdalene, she is acting out of her appreciation that Jesus has set her free. This freedom allows her to stand under Jesus when he is on the cross, when all the disciples except John are in hiding for fear of their lives.

I wrote the following poem after working with a woman named Lisa who talked about learning "the trade of the tricks." It struck me as such a perfect phrasing for the craziness of the world she was coming from. The poem sums up some thoughts about ways in which the commitment we are making to our Lord is completely freeing, not binding. As we spend the next few days studying about Magdalene, maybe this poem can help us celebrate the fact that all of us can be saints and help us imagine ways we can offer our best to the Lord, who frees us and makes us incredibly rich.

The Trade of the Tricks

It's backwards on the streets.
Nothing is what it seems.
What looks like the ticket to wealth is the gate to poverty.
It seems lucky out there if they drop you off close to town after they rape you,
So you don't have to walk so far.
It's just the trade of the tricks
to make you feel cheap.

It's all backwards in the Gospels.
Nothing is what it seems.
What seems like the ticket to ruin is the path to bliss.
It seems miraculous in here that in giving it all up,
you become priceless
So you're free to love whom you choose because
you are worth the world.
It's just the trick of the priests' trade,
to make grace feel cheap.

Reflecting and Recording

What is an example of a grace-filled paradox that you have found to be true in your spiritual journey?

What does the word *surrender* mean to you?

Can you think of a turn of phrase that would describe a truth in your life, a truth that may seem crazy to the world?

Prayer

Almighty God, whose blessed Son restored Mary Magdalene to health of body and of mind, and called her to be a witness of his resurrection: Mercifully grant that by your grace we may be healed from all our infirmities and know you in the power of his unending life. Amen.

DAY THREE: HOW JESUS RELATES TO WOMEN IN THE GOSPELS

John 4:13-15

Jesus said to her, "Everyone who drinks of this water will be thirsty again, but those who drink of the water that I will give them will never be thirsty. The water that I will give will become in them a spring of water gushing up to eternal life." The woman said to him, "Sir, give me this water, so that I may never be thirsty or have to keep coming here to draw water."

John 8:3-11

The scribes and the Pharisees brought a woman who had been caught in adultery; and making her stand before all of them, they said to him, "Teacher, this woman was caught in the very act of committing adultery. Now in the law Moses commanded us to stone such women. Now what do you say?" They said this to test him, so that they might have some charge to bring against him. Jesus bent down and wrote with his finger on the ground. When they kept on questioning him, he straightened up and said to them, "Let anyone among you who is without sin be the first to throw a stone at her." And once again he bent down and wrote on the ground. When they heard it, they went away, one by one, beginning with the elders; and Jesus was left alone with the woman standing before him. Jesus straightened up and said to her, "Woman, where are they? Has no one condemned you?" She said, "No one, sir." And Jesus said, "Neither do I condemn you. Go your way, and from now on do not sin again."

These are just two of the wonderful examples of the intimate and compassionate way that Jesus related to women in the Gospels. He saw them as God created them, as full human beings reflecting the image of God. The story of his encounters with women is an important aspect of the good news that Jesus proclaims to the world. He knows that in a new Kingdom where the last shall be first, women are vital to the vision. In our two stories today, for example, Jesus sees clearly who the women are and what it will take to set them free.

As it says in 2 Corinthians 3:18, "And all of us, with unveiled faces, seeing the glory of the Lord as though reflected in a mirror, are being transformed into the same image from one degree of glory to another; for this comes from the Lord, the Spirit." If one of the points of writing the Scriptures was so that humanity would know the reconciling love of God in Christ, then it is critical that Jesus reach out and share that message with females, who represent half of the human population. Among the Gospels, John's is unique in the way it unfolds the story of Jesus, filling the story with wonderful metaphors and language laden with love. His inclusion of women in the unfolding of the story fits with these themes, as the women are open and eager to hear his compassionate message.

It seems that Jesus delights in the encounters he has with women. He communicates well with them, sees them as worthy matches for verbal games, knows they are creative, and finds joy and satisfaction in relationships with them. Jesus takes women seriously, knowing that they are responsible for their actions and that they know the difference between godly relationships and using their bodies at the cost of their souls.

The woman at the well and the woman caught in adultery are good examples of the way Jesus' love and grace extend beyond the normal Judaic laws concerning women and the fact that all people who desire to forgive others as they have been forgiven are welcome in the circle. That is why it is likely that Magdalene was part of the circle of believers who traveled with Jesus. She wasn't excluded from Jesus' ministry for being a woman, and neither are we.

The message for us is that Jesus has a vital part for us to play as co-workers in the Kingdom in whatever way we are able to use our talents to serve him. We are capable of doing great evangelism, serving the local church, prophesying, and teaching God's Word. Jesus wants each woman to give herself to him in utter dependence, knowing that without him we can do nothing. We need to rely on the Holy Spirit to fulfill our special ministry. Isaiah says that each of us has been called by name from our mother's womb to fulfill God's purpose for our lives.

If you feel inadequate in the ministry to which God has called you, remember Jesus' words as Paul relates them in 2 Corinthians 12:9: "My grace is sufficient for you, for power is made perfect in weakness." In every glimpse we have of Magdalene, we see her acting out of appreciation for what Jesus had done in setting her free. Magdalene loved the Lord and wanted to serve him, and her obedience flowed from that love. For us to be obedient we must listen to the word of God, not just by listening and considering what we hear but by putting faith into action so it is a positive, active response.

Magdalene's faith was not complicated; she was more eager to believe and obey than to understand. Sometimes in our lives, things happen that we don't understand; and we must stand strong and continue to believe and obey Jesus. Magdalene's devoted faithfulness to Jesus and her announcement of Christ's victory over death shouts to women everywhere that an encounter with Jesus changes life forever. She personifies the many women for whom Jesus has demonstrated his depth of love, mercy, and forgiveness.

Is it too much to believe that Mary Magdalene was a woman who yearned for love that enhanced rather than dominated, that stretched her instead of diminishing her, that inspired her to take risks rather than leaving her frightened and apologizing for her talents? It is not difficult to imagine what attracted her to a man like Jesus. Surrounded by followers who had abandoned everything to work with Jesus in achieving his vision, she found herself caught up in a movement bent on offering the world a new definition of love, community, and family. The motley band of followers who gathered around this charismatic teacher was drawn to his utopian vision of a beloved community, one not marred by the divisiveness of hierarchy, prejudice, bigotry, self-righteousness, lust, and power. Despite the many examples in the Gospels where they missed the point or reverted back to traditional thinking, Jesus' disciples wanted to believe in this new world he offered them. They were drawn to the Carpenter because they wanted to believe it was possible to live and love differently from the way they had been taught. For a thinking woman of faith, here was the answer to a prayer.

In our readings and reflections on Magdalene, we are encouraged to remember that we have been given all we need to live our lives with depth, sincerity, and hope. It is not that we lack anything to live well and faithfully; we just don't always remember that we are made in the image of God, beautiful and whole.

Reflecting and Recording

Do you look beyond people's social standing and see them as equal in the kingdom of God?

Do you see yourself as being called by God?

If you had to imagine yourself as one of the women in the Gospel of John who encounters Jesus, which one would you be?

Prayer

Lord, make me an instrument of your peace; where there is hatred, let me sow love; where there is injury, pardon; where there is doubt, faith; where there is despair, hope; where there is darkness, light; and where there is sadness, joy. Grant that I may not so much seek to be consoled as to console; to be understood, as to understand; to be loved, as to love; for it is in giving that we receive, it is in pardoning that we are pardoned, and it is in dying that we are born to eternal life. Amen.

(Attributed to Francis of Assisi, 13th century)

DAY FOUR: MORALITY IS GRATITUDE

I was walking up a beautiful hillside in the woods of Tennessee with a friend who is a priest. It was the kind of warm fall day when the trees look as though they have been lit up for a festival. The orange maples, the yellow tulip poplars, and the red dogwoods put me in mind of God's abundant love for us. The scene made us both aware of the sacredness of life.

Several times over the past decade my friend has asked me where I find myself in the Scriptures. He always says that we have to ground ourselves in the story, and then we can see where we need to go. He has worked with the homeless for over twenty years and has stayed as devoted and committed to his work as anyone I have ever known. I trust his spiritual direction and wanted to know how he had been able to live out his faith in a way so devoted and dedicated.

And so on that walk I asked him if he could sum up his faith for me. He said, "Life is a gift; morality is gratitude." He went on to tell me that he learned that from his mentor some twenty-five years before and that it had proven to be a good mantra by which to live a life of servant ministry.

We first must know that our life is a gift from God. Everything we have is a gift, and everything we are able to do is a gift. In this light our morality is not a burden in which laws are imposed on us. It does not restrict our ability to do what we desire. It is a response to a loving God, who loved us first. In all the examples in the Gospel of John, what Jesus offered the women was an opportunity to live morally, so that devotion and gratitude were an offering for the great gift they had been given. How much happier our world would be if we could live that way, doing the right thing out of gratitude instead of duty.

If all our opportunities to feed the hungry, clothe the naked, give drink to the thirsty, go to prison, care for the sick, and bury the dead are seen as chances to show our gratitude, I think we would live more joyful lives. Sometimes we see such opportunities as a drain on time that we think is our own, when in fact they allow us to offer back to God thanks for what is God's. This way of seeing things changes the mood of our reflections on duty and devotion. It transforms our opportunities to serve and to love into means of showing gratitude to God.

Mary Magdalene lived with a deep sense of gratitude that made her moral and free. In her encounter with Jesus she saw that her life was a gift. All the devotion, love, and faithfulness she demonstrated after that was simply gratitude for that gift. I wonder, when she was at the cross and at the tomb on Easter morning, if she ever felt that those tasks were a burden. I suspect instead that they were a natural response to her love of Jesus and that she would not have wanted to be anywhere else. There have been many nights when I have gotten up with a sick child or have had to run to the hospital to offer last rites to a dying patient. I pray that I can be more like Mary Magdalene and see these "inconveniences" as blessings. Through this study I am reminded that, truly, it is not my time or my sleep that I am sacrificing. It is all an offering to God. The balance comes from bearing it all more joyfully and making the space in our lives to be open to those experiences.

Reflecting and Recording

Where do you find yourself in the Scriptures? If you had to be one character in the Gospels, which one would you choose?

Can you sum up your faith in a sentence that you can use as a guide in your daily living?

Prayer

Loving God, give us the joy of filling our days with ways to serve you, care for others, and tend to ourselves, all in gratitude for the love that we know in you. Amen.

DAY FIVE: THEY WERE THERE TO ANOINT HIM

Matthew 27:55–28:15

Many women were also there, looking on from a distance; they had followed Jesus
from Galilee and had provided for him. Among them were Mary Magdalene,
and Mary the mother of James and Joseph, and the mother of the sons of Zebedee.
When it was evening, there came a rich man from Arimathea,
named Joseph, who was also a disciple of Jesus.
He went to Pilate and asked for the body of Jesus; then Pilate ordered it
to be given to him. So Joseph took the body and wrapped it in a clean linen cloth
and laid it in his own new tomb, which he had hewn in the rock.
He then rolled a great stone to the door of the tomb and went away.
Mary Magdalene and the other Mary were there, sitting opposite the tomb.
The next day, that is, after the day of Preparation, the chief priests
and the Pharisees gathered before Pilate and said,
"Sir, we remember what that impostor said while he was still alive,
'After three days I will rise again.' Therefore command the tomb to be made secure
until the third day; otherwise his disciples may go and steal him away,
and tell the people, 'He has been raised from the dead,'
and the last deception would be worse than the first." Pilate said to them,
"You have a guard of soldiers; go, make it as secure as you can."
So they went with the guard and made the tomb secure by sealing the stone.
After the sabbath, as the first day of the week was dawning,
Mary Magdalene and the other Mary went to see the tomb.

And suddenly there was a great earthquake; for an angel of the Lord,
descending from heaven, came and rolled back the stone and sat on it.
His appearance was like lightning, and his clothing white as snow.
For fear of him the guards shook and became like dead men.
But the angel said to the women, "Do not be afraid; I know that you are looking
for Jesus who was crucified. He is not here; for he has been raised, as he said.
Come, see the place where he lay. Then go quickly and tell his disciples,
'He has been raised from the dead, and indeed he is going ahead of you to Galilee;
there you will see him.' This is my message for you."
So they left the tomb quickly with fear and great joy, and ran to tell his disciples.
Suddenly, Jesus met them and said, "Greetings!"
And they came to him, took hold of his feet, and worshiped him.
Then Jesus said to them, "Do not be afraid;
go and tell my brothers to go to Galilee; there they will see me."
While they were going, some of the guard went into the city
and told the chief priests everything that had happened.
After the priests had assembled with the elders, they devised a plan
to give a large sum of money to the soldiers, telling them, "You must say,
'His disciples came by night and stole him away while we were asleep.'
If this comes to the governor's ears, we will satisfy him and keep you out of trouble."
So they took the money and did as they were directed.
And this story is still told among the Jews to this day.

The story of Mary Magdalene as being present at Jesus' tomb appears in all the Gospels. During the last two days of study this week, we will consider two of those accounts.

In today's account from Matthew, it strikes me that the faithful women, women who were devoted and knew their duty, were the ones bringing spices to anoint the body of Jesus. This would indicate that they were not expecting a resurrection; they were just caring for the man whom they loved. Mary Magdalene and Mary the mother of James were some of the faithful few to stand at a distance during the Crucifixion (in John's Gospel they are closer), and they were brave enough to follow Joseph of Arimathea in the presence of the Roman army to see where the body would be taken.

Mary Magdalene was the first one in this Gospel to visit the tomb on Easter morning, and so she was the one who heard the news first, that Jesus had indeed risen from the dead. In this telling, the news of the Resurrection from an angel causes a great earthquake; and the angel sits upon the rolled stone. What a great message of triumph! The same stone that was used to seal Jesus in his grave is now used to proclaim the Resurrection. In all our lives, the great stones that might seal our deaths turn out to be the very places where we can see, hear, and feel resurrection. Magdalene, weeping and weary from carrying all the spices, must have been filled with joy to find that her Lord lived.

Two thousand years later, one of the great lessons for us is that if we are faithful in love, we will see resurrection in places that we thought were dead. Like the women carrying the spices to care for the body, we are called simply to be faithful and devoted; and we will see the living God acting in our lives.

The women are present not just as mourners but as witnesses to the living God. It is of no small consequence, given that their testimony would have had little value under Jewish law, that our whole heritage as Christians rests in their telling of the events at the tomb that morning. What they described was enough to scare the chief priests into paying off the guards to tell a different story, as the priests tried to suppress the truth of what the women had seen. The priests thought they could use their power to appease the governor. What they didn't count on was that the truth would be told over and over again, even though it could have cost the disciples their lives, and that it would spread and change the entire world.

The message is clear for us. We are armed with that same truth. If we can speak it clearly to those close to us, the message of resurrection will continue to live through us. Like our foremothers, Mary Magdalene and the other Mary, we can proclaim in our words and lives what we have seen and what we know to be true about God. It is the way for us to offer ourselves in duty and devotion to our Lord. It is the way to live with our hearts and minds in union, bearing witness to the message of resurrection.

This doesn't mean we have to stand on rocks and shout, "He is risen!" It also doesn't mean that our job is to try and convert others to what we believe. It does mean that in our daily actions we preach the truth of our risen Lord, who loves the entire world—his people and his creation. Francis of Assisi said that we are to preach love always and, when necessary, use words. Moreover, as my mother said, treat everyone like they were the Son of God.

Reflecting and Recording

When have you seen life where you thought you would find death?

Who has shown you new life in the last year?

What is the best way for you to preach about resurrection in your life?

Prayer

O Lord, you have given us the grace to know the resurrection of your Son. Grant that the Holy Spirit may raise us to newness of life this day. Amen.

DAY SIX: JESUS LINGERS FOR MAGDALENE AT THE TOMB

John 20:1-18

Early on the first day of the week, while it was still dark,
Mary Magdalene came to the tomb and saw that the stone had been removed
from the tomb. So she ran and went to Simon Peter and the other disciple,
the one whom Jesus loved, and said to them,
"They have taken the Lord out of the tomb, and we do not know
where they have laid him." Then Peter and the other disciple set out
and went toward the tomb. The two were running together, but the other disciple
outran Peter and reached the tomb first. He bent down to look in
and he saw the linen wrappings lying there, but he did not go in.
Then Simon Peter came, following him, and went into the tomb.
He saw the linen wrappings lying there, and the cloth that had been
on Jesus' head, not lying with the linen wrappings but rolled up in a place by itself.
Then the other disciple, who reached the tomb first, also went in,
and he saw and believed; for as yet they did not understand the scripture,
that he must rise from the dead. Then the disciples returned to their homes.
But Mary stood weeping outside the tomb. As she wept, she bent over
to look into the tomb; and she saw two angels in white, sitting where the body
of Jesus had been lying, one at the head and the other at the feet.
They said to her, "Woman, why are you weeping?" She said to them,
"They have taken away my Lord, and I do not know where they have laid him."
When she said this, she turned round and saw Jesus standing there,
but she did not know that it was Jesus. Jesus said to her,

"Woman, why are you weeping? Whom are you looking for?"
Supposing him to be the gardener, she said to him,
"Sir, if you have carried him away, tell me where you have laid him,
and I will take him away."
Jesus said to her, "Mary!" She turned and said to him in Hebrew, "Rabbouni!"
(which means Teacher). Jesus said to her, "Do not hold on to me,
because I have not yet ascended to the Father. But go to my brothers
and say to them, 'I am ascending to my Father and your Father, to my God
and your God.' " Mary Magdalene went and announced to the disciples,
"I have seen the Lord"; and she told them that he had said these things to her.

The highest honor given to anyone in the Gospels is given to Mary Magdalene. She is the first person to proclaim the Resurrection. She is the preacher to the preacher and the first one to proclaim the good news: "He is risen."

In this telling of the Resurrection in the Gospel of John, we are given an intimate and detailed description of the events on the third day. Magdalene was at the tomb at first light that resurrection morning. She seemed completely surprised and scared that the stone had been rolled away. Looking into the cave, she saw that it was empty, and it made her weep. She rushed to find John and Peter and blurted out, "They have taken away the Lord out of the tomb, and we know not where they have laid him."

John and Peter, the two disciples who raced to the tomb and came in first and second, didn't see the angels or Jesus by the shroud. They ran in and saw the linen lying there, and they ran back to their homes. But Magdalene, who probably came in a distant third behind the two disciples, stood outside the tomb and wept, still grieving and searching for a sign. She bent over and looked once more into the tomb, where she saw the two angels in white. It must have been hard to see them, or else how could John and Peter, who were trying to be faithful, have missed them? Either the angels were hiding from the disciples, appeared after the disciples left, or were waiting for Magdalene. Then, just as she saw them, another person appeared to her and asked why she was weeping. Most of us would react the way John and Peter did. We would see something we don't fully understand and run away before discovering the real treasure awaiting us. John and Peter's hasty retreat caused them to miss the Lord in their midst.

Too often the same thing happens to us. We begin searching our hearts and minds for answers in our faith, and as soon as we see any evidence of new life, we run away, missing the greater lessons waiting for us. A good example of this is in relationships. The rush of feelings overwhelms us when we first fall in love. When those feelings begin to change into something else, we sometimes get scared and run away. But if we can stay together, loving each other and honoring each other, there is a love experienced that no new relationship can touch. It is a love born of a willingness to stand outside the tomb and weep and look into it again.

Two years ago, I went to Hawaii with my husband. A friend was getting married and asked us to come perform the ceremony and sing. During the six days on that island paradise, I kept wondering how I could experience such joy in my marriage. The answer was that my husband and I found our way to God through our relationship. I was so thankful we both kept lingering at the tomb, because if either of us had chosen to run, I would have missed that feeling.

The next part of the Resurrection story in John is much more intimate, and the only person there to tell what transpired was Mary Magdalene. After John and Peter left, we witness the miraculous story of how the Resurrection first came to light for humanity. In her grief and love, Magdalene saw the angels and begged them to show her the body. While others were already racing back to report the new developments, she sat in the empty tomb and wept. When Jesus appeared to her, she didn't turn away; and when he called her name, she recognized him. Thus it is that a foreign, sinful woman was the first person to see the risen Jesus. Her experience shows that, for any of us, seeing the risen Lord is a privileged gift. What makes us worthy of the gift? Our hearts and our faithfulness.

In this account, it is as if Jesus was waiting for her. He told her he was ascending and directed her to go and tell the news to the disciples. She left, knowing that in all the world she was the one to have seen the risen Lord. What an awesome gift and responsibility! I wonder if all the pieces started fitting together for her as she left to tell the disciples. We will never know, because her story ends there. We are left to wonder where she went for the rest of her ministry. The story leaves us with many questions. Why didn't John and Peter see Jesus? Why did Jesus wait for Mary Magdalene? How was her life changed, knowing that she had sat with the risen Lord?

For me, it was Magdalene's ultimate sense of duty and devotion that made it possible for her to participate in the Resurrection. It was Magdalene who wept at the cross, who experienced forgiveness, who in another Gospel set the scene for reminding the disciples that the poor would always be with them. It was Magdalene who, on Easter morning, was coming to anoint the Lord she loved. Most of us, like John and Peter, are blind. It is easy to miss the Lord even when he stands beside us, at our feet, even within us. Most of the time we miss him, but every now and then we are graced with Magdalene's gift. If we want to see the face of God, we must be willing to go to the empty tomb and sit and weep and wait.

Reflecting and Recording

Why do you think that Jesus didn't show himself to John or Peter?

Have you ever witnessed the miracle of resurrection in your own life?

Prayer

You are gracious in your forgetting, Lord. Thank you for the gift of freedom so that what I once was is not who I am today. I can live freely in your forgiveness and walk in your light. Amen.

DAY SEVEN: PREPARING FOR GROUP DISCUSSION

Mary's Quatrain

I give to you my tender flesh,
Carved out of my old brokenness,
Offer it as my holy sin,
And wail and wait for resurrection.

The Beloved's Refrain

Inside this stone my heart is beating.
Woman, tell me, why are you weeping?

Week Six:
The Anointings
of Jesus Christ

DAY ONE: THE FORGOTTEN SACRAMENT

John 13:3-5, 12-17

Jesus . . . got up from the table, took off his outer robe, and tied a towel
around himself. Then he poured water into a basin and began to wash
the disciples' feet and to wipe them with the towel that was tied around him. . . .
After he had washed their feet, had put on his robe, and had returned to the table,
he said to them, "Do you know what I have done to you?
You call me Teacher and Lord—and you are right, for that is what I am.
So if I, your Lord and Teacher, have washed your feet, you also ought
to wash one another's feet. For I have set you an example, that you also should do
as I have done to you. Very truly, I tell you, servants are not greater
than their master, nor are messengers greater than the one
who sent them. If you know these things, you are blessed if you do them."

The quintessential union of duty and devotion is found in foot washing. It is the embodiment of servant ministry and is the one thing in the Scriptures that Jesus asks us to do if we call ourselves his disciples. For our last week together, it is a fitting theme.

The image of Jesus taking off his outer coat, putting on a towel, and kneeling before his disciples is so humbling. At the same time, it shows why we call Jesus our Lord and try to follow in his footsteps. The love he demonstrates for the disciples is the kind of love we seek to show one another.

There is a practical and a ritualistic side to foot washing. The practical side is that feet are dirty. The disciples had traveled down dusty roads in sandals, and by evening their feet needed a good washing. In fact, they had walked for the better part of three years with Jesus. I imagine it felt wonderful for people with callused and achy feet to have someone wash their feet.

Foot washing is also a profound ritual. It honors the receiver, and it signifies that the person is cleansed. There is a trace of this ritual left in the liturgy of the Episcopal Church. Just before the priest holds the bread and wine in the presentation of the Eucharist, someone will offer a small bowl and towel to the priest, who then places his or her hands over the bowl as the server pours water over them. It's easier and less intimate to wash someone's hands than feet, but I think the idea of cleansing is what has remained.

I have tried to make foot washings part of my practice in recent years—mostly to keep in mind that servanthood needs to be central in my ministry, but also because I have found that when people allow you to wash their feet, it is a holy moment. The entire community of folks associated with Magdalene participates in foot washings. The way the ritual is practiced in our circle is that we sit in silence, and one at a time we take a small bit of our "Balm of Gilead" to use on one another's feet. Balm of Gilead is the body balm (made of olive oil, beeswax, and almond oil) that we make in our cottage industry, Thistle Farms. It is the first product we produced and is an outward and visible sign of healing that we have found internally through the work of Magdalene. In our practice, one person kneels before another's feet, wipes them off with a clean towel, and then rubs the oils into the feet with a silent prayer for that person. That person then gets up, goes to someone else, kneels, and starts the process again.

I use foot washing in other areas of my life as well. We have held foot-washing circles during mission trips from my church to a community in Ecuador. A photograph taken on one of those trips a couple of years ago shows a circle of feet in every stage and walk of life. It is a beautiful reminder of how washing one another's feet can bring us closer and into a new fellowship. In my church we use a modified foot-washing ceremony each year at our Holy Thursday service, before we begin a prayer vigil that carries us into Good Friday. At a recent Thanksgiving family gathering, I brought some of the balm with me. The Friday after Thanksgiving is a kind of a pampering time in my family, where daughters and nieces sit around doing nails, putting on facial masks, and braiding hair. I asked my ten-year-old niece if she wanted some of the balm on her hands or feet. "Well, my feet are pretty dirty; so I guess you better do them," she answered.

Foot washing has been called the forgotten sacrament. We baptize people and offer each other Communion, but it is not a regular part of our Christian liturgies to wash each other's feet. It is interesting in a community founded on Jesus' words ("I have set you an example that you should do as I have done") that we no longer maintain this practice. Henri Nouwen, a wonderful theologian who moved into a community in the 1980s to serve people with mental illness, began to make foot washing a part of the regular weekly activities. He said that it changed the nature of how those in the community served one another. The caregivers allowed the people they cared for to wash their feet, and then they exchanged places. It humbled and bonded the entire community. It gave all the participants a sense of the honor that comes to those who are willing to serve. It also gave a sense of real appreciation for all the work the caregivers offer during the week.

I believe that in trying to be balanced in our faith, kneeling to wash our brothers' and sisters' feet keeps us grounded. In addition to Jesus' example offered to us in John, each Gospel records that Jesus was anointed or had his feet washed by a woman. We have already read one of those passages, from the seventh chapter of Luke, when we studied Mary Magdalene. In the Gospel of Mark, the anointing occurs in the fourteenth chapter, immediately following Jesus' teaching and the widow's offering. In the Gospel of John it occurs in the twelfth chapter, as the family of Mary and Martha return to the spotlight. In Matthew it takes place in the twenty-sixth chapter, and as in Mark it is Jesus' head that is anointed rather than his feet.

Some theologians speculate that all the recorded anointings of Jesus were the same event, told differently by different authors; but others say that these events occurred at different times and places and signified different things. All four Gospels mention Jesus being anointed by a woman. Whereas the feeding of the five thousand is mentioned in all four Gospels, with remarkably few differing perspectives, the anointings of Jesus by women are all told somewhat differently. It is likely that more than one woman showed this expression of new life in Christ on more than one occasion.

Reflecting and Recording

Today I offer you an activity instead of a question. Go and wash someone's feet and use it as a time of prayer.

Prayer

Jesus, in your tender love for us, you gave examples of how to serve one another. Give us another day to love each other as you have loved us. Amen.

DAY TWO: THE MONEY COULD BE SPENT ON THE POOR

Matthew 26:6-13

*Now while Jesus was at Bethany in the house of Simon the leper, a woman
came to him with an alabaster jar of very costly ointment, and she poured it
on his head as he sat at table. But when the disciples saw it, they were angry
and said, "Why this waste? For this ointment could have been sold for a large sum,
and the money given to the poor." But Jesus, aware of this, said to them,
"Why do you trouble the woman? She has done a good service for me.
For you always have the poor with you, but you will not always have me.
By pouring this ointment on my body she has prepared me for burial.
Truly, I tell you, wherever this good news is proclaimed in the whole world,
what she has done will be told in remembrance of her."*

Matthew, Mark, and John tell of an anointing that occurred just before the
Passover. In all three of these accounts, women are the ones anointing Jesus and
thus providing the means by which Jesus proclaims the miracle of forgiveness,
generosity, and freedom.

In Matthew's account the woman had an expensive ointment that she poured
on his head. This is worth noting in itself. While anointing the head can be part
of the preparation for burial, it is also a sign of royal commission. It meant that
in this case the woman took on the role of a prophet. What seemed to offend
the disciples was that using expensive oil was a waste of money, not that the
practice itself was out of the ordinary or strange. The disciples' rationale was
that the oil could have been sold and the money given to the poor.

131

A modern-day example of this story comes from one of the feeding homes that was run by Dorothy Day in the 1960s. The story goes that a woman came in and handed Dorothy Day a large, beautiful diamond ring. Day thanked the woman; then she turned around and handed it to a lonely old woman who often came to eat a meal. That evening, Day's staff questioned her about her extravagant actions. By selling the ring at a diamond exchange, there would have been enough money to buy a month's worth of groceries for a thousand people. Day told her staff that she did what she thought was right. Then she asked, "Do you suppose that God created diamonds only for the rich?" She noted that the woman had her dignity, and that the woman "could sell it if she liked and spend the money for rent, a trip to the Bahamas, or keep the ring to admire." (*Dorothy Day: Selected Writings*, edited by Robert Ellsberg; Orbis, 1992; introduction)

I was privileged to witness another modern-day example during a family trip to Washington, DC. A man was sitting on the steps in front of the Museum of Natural History, jingling a cup, hoping for change from tourists. My husband dropped in some coins as we were walking up the stairs; and my middle son, Caney, must have noticed this act. After we looked at the dinosaurs and the precious gems, we went to the gift store, where each boy was allowed to buy a memento. Caney picked a small coiled snake made of stone that he thought was really great. Our two other sons bought stones. When we headed out the door, Caney saw that the man was still sitting there, shaking his cup. Caney stopped and thought for a long minute, then put his stone snake in the cup. The man didn't say anything but sort of shook his head as if to tell Caney it wasn't necessary. My husband said, "Caney, you didn't have to do that. He can't use it anyway." Caney answered, "He can use it as much as I can." Then his two brothers, seeing how kind Caney had been, gave Caney their stones. So Caney, who had given away his memento, ended up with two. It was so simple and beautiful. Caney had given something that to him was lavish, not because it was the best utilitarian use of our goods, but because he thought it was valuable and would be a great offering.

The passage in Matthew gives us permission to be lavish in our giving to those we cherish. We don't always have to think about what is the best use of our resources or whether have we spent all that we have; sometimes we can just pour out gifts upon others because we love them, and that can be a blessing by God. Oftentimes at Magdalene we step in when someone is in a financial bind and give money. One woman complained, saying that it wasn't fair. I repeated the words I heard my mother say as I was growing up, "When did I promise you fair?" It is not fair, and that is what makes it a gift.

Reflecting and Recording

Do you ever put a price on your devotion, above what you think your duty is worth?

Can you think of a gift that you have been given that you would consider lavish?

Prayer

Give us grace this day to love what you love, Jesus, and to desire what you desire more than all the wealth this world can offer. Amen.

DAY THREE: PREPARING FOR BURIAL

John 12:1-8

Six days before the Passover Jesus came to Bethany, the home of Lazarus, whom [Jesus] had raised from the dead. There they gave a dinner for him. Martha served, and Lazarus was one of those at the table with him. Mary took a pound of costly perfume made of pure nard, anointed Jesus' feet, and wiped them with her hair. The house was filled with the fragrance of the perfume. But Judas Iscariot, one of his disciples (the one who was about to betray him), said, "Why was this perfume not sold for three hundred denarii and the money given to the poor?" (He said this not because he cared about the poor, but because he was a thief; he kept the common purse and used to steal what was put into it.) Jesus said, "Leave her alone. She bought it so that she might keep it for the day of my burial. You always have the poor with you, but you do not always have me."

This version of the anointing comes immediately after Jesus had raised Mary and Martha's brother from the dead. It is easy to imagine the gratitude and love that Mary and Martha felt toward Jesus. In many ways this story of the anointing is similar to Mark's. It also seems to draw some details from Luke's account—for example, the meal setting and the fact that the woman anointed Jesus' feet and dried them with her hair. It is worth noting that it is Mary, not Martha, who served Jesus. Mary, the one who had sat and listened at his feet, the one who Jesus said chose the better path, was the one who took a great deal of costly ointment and bathed Jesus' feet in it, wiping them with her hair. What

134

is unique in John's Gospel is that Judas Iscariot appears in contrast to the woman, crying out on behalf of the poor. We know that Judas betrayed Jesus within days of this story; thus, we might conclude that his protest had less to do with his generous spirit toward the poor than with his problems with Jesus.

I have found similar parallels in my church ministry. Many times people get upset when money is spent on things to make the church beautiful, saying that it is scandalous in light of the number of homeless people in our midst. While I can see their point of view, for the most part these are not the people starting fundraising campaigns to support the homeless ministries. Instead, these ministries typically just get a line item in the regular budget of the congregation. When we complain about the money we spend on something, is it usually because we would rather not be generous with that money or just want to keep it for ourselves. In balancing our faith, it is good to remember how much or how little we honestly do lavish on the poor in honor of God.

What is beautiful about the account in John is that Mary did what she could for Jesus. She offered him the very best and spared no expense or even decorum. In her great act of humility and thanksgiving, she did even more than she realized. She didn't seem to spare anything in her action. Jesus' ministry saved her brother and changed her life, and she appears no longer to be constrained by practicality or by the financial and material implications of her actions. Her vision was far greater than that. Her vision was for the glory of God and for the worship of her Savior. Jesus knew her heart and saw a generous act that gave him honor. She did it in a time when his ministry was causing political problems and when he was risking much by proclaiming the new Kingdom.

What Mary did has to be messy and maybe even a little embarrassing—using a pound of nard ointment that surely had spilled onto Martha's clean floor, mingling with her hair. But to those who witnessed the act and were overcome by the powerful fragrance filling the house, it was a wondrous story that had to be told. Then there is Judas, looking at this overwhelming display of gratitude and love, who judged Mary and missed the point of her actions. In the eyes of God it is Judas who was far from the heart of God's kingdom. God knows our hearts and our desire to honor God's blessings. Whenever we do deeds with heart and intention, God is honored.

Reflection and Recording

Have you developed a heart so free that nothing holds you back from being the person God wants you to be?

What do you think of what Mary did? Do you admire it as Jesus did? Or is there something of Judas in you?

What was it that Jesus admired in Mary?

Prayer

Holy and life-giving Spirit, teach us how to serve you and others with the pureness of heart that Mary had, as she washed your feet and dried them with her hair. Amen.

DAY FOUR: TEARS FOR CLEANSING

Mark 14:3-9

While he was at Bethany in the house of Simon the leper, as he sat at the table,
a woman came with an alabaster jar of very costly ointment of nard,
and she broke open the jar and poured the ointment on his head.
But some were there who said to one another in anger, "Why was the ointment
wasted in this way? For this ointment could have been sold
for more than three hundred denarii, and the money given to the poor."
And they scolded her. But Jesus said, "Let her alone; why do you trouble her?
She has performed a good service for me. For you always have the poor with you,
and you can show kindness to them whenever you wish;
but you will not always have me. She has done what she could;
she has anointed my body beforehand for its burial.
Truly I tell you, wherever the good news is proclaimed in the whole world,
what she has done will be told in remembrance of her."

Luke 7:36-39

One of the Pharisees asked Jesus to eat with him, and he went
into the Pharisee's house and took his place at the table. And a woman in the city,
who was a sinner, having learned that he was eating in the Pharisee's house,
brought an alabaster jar of ointment. She stood behind him at his feet, weeping,
and began to bathe his feet with her tears and to dry them with her hair.
Then she continued kissing his feet and anointing them with the ointment.

Now when the Pharisee who had invited him saw it, he said to himself,
"If this man were a prophet, he would have known
who and what kind of woman this is who is touching him—that she is a sinner."

The account in the Gospel of Mark is in some ways the clearest for me. There was a meal, and an uninvited woman offered Jesus the greatest offering of hospitality. There were people who responded in anger to her offering and wanted Jesus to praise them for their insight and practicality. Instead Jesus praised the woman's act, and it became symbolic of forgiveness and kindness.

We have already looked at Luke's account, but let's revisit the story for a minute in this setting. Let's learn again from the woman with no name who preached the gospel, not in words but in action. Luke's story is about a religious man called a Pharisee, and we are not given the reason for his invitation to Jesus. All we know is that the Pharisee invited Jesus to dinner, and Jesus came. Maybe the Pharisee just wanted to spend some time with this Galilean. But, as a Pharisee and a man of religion, he did not even offer his guest the normal kindnesses. He didn't wash Jesus' feet. He didn't provide water. He didn't offer Jesus the kiss of greeting.

We know that in those days there were such things as private dinners and public dinners; and I'm assuming this was a kind of public dinner. Maybe the Pharisee was showing off his guest. Maybe the front door was open; but for some reason the sinner from the street felt she could come in and observe the dinner. In those days people did not sit in chairs around a table as we do. The tables were very low, so the dinner guest and host sat or reclined on the floor. In our story we can imagine that the feet of the guests were fanned out around the table, and the woman from the streets found her way to Jesus' feet and began to weep. The adjective used to describe her is *sinful*. In the Greek it's actually a noun, so this woman is actually called "a sinner" or "the sinner."

In both Mark's and Luke's Gospels, the woman proceeded to do something that shocked the religious leaders surrounding Jesus. In Mark, she broke open a jar and poured it on his head, similar to what the woman did in Matthew. In Luke she cried and fell at his feet, kissing them and demonstrating more affection than was in any way customary for Jesus to allow. Then she did something that was almost unforgivable in those days, and indeed in much of Eastern society today: she unfurled her hair in public. She unfurled her hair and began to wipe the feet of Jesus with it—something unthinkable. In biblical times, women wore a flask around their neck containing precious oil used for the most special of occasions. With the fragrant oil, which she probably had purchased using money made on the streets, the woman anointed the feet of Jesus.

In these Gospel accounts, Jesus used the women's actions as occasions to talk about the nature of forgiveness and what was to come for him. What is our lesson? Perhaps we should admit that we don't have all the answers, that we are still sinners and should simply be grateful. Or we can reflect on the actions of those involved and try to learn something from our responses. On one hand, we might feel ourselves responding like the Pharisee and Simon the leper. While it makes sense that the Pharisee has some arrogance in his understanding of protocol and would be offended, it seems that Simon the leper would have more sympathy for the woman and a deeper sense of gratitude toward Jesus. In any event, if we offer very little forgiveness, as they did, then that is all the forgiveness we will receive. But if we can find a way in our hearts to respond more like the woman who anointed Jesus, showing duty and devotion in a beautiful way, then we can experience untold forgiveness and mercy.

Jesus teaches that when we don't think we need much forgiveness, we won't have the capacity to show much love for the one who forgives. When we realize how desperately we need forgiveness, our love will be in proportion to our joy in being forgiven. Jesus said, "Woman, your sins are forgiven; go in peace"; but he never said anything to Simon about forgiveness. In our study about living a balanced life of duty and devotion, the Scriptures this week teach us that the more we can offer our hearts, the fuller they will become. This doesn't mean we should run around serving everyone until we are exhausted; instead, it means adopting the attitude of the women in the stories, whose desire it was to serve God with their lives. Whether we are studying Scripture, raising our children, going on retreat, or serving the homeless, we can do all this with an open and loving heart.

The story in Mark ends by saying that the act was so generous that it will be remembered everywhere in the world where people honor goodness. The story in Luke ends with Jesus saying to the woman, "Your faith has saved you; go in peace." This is the kind of pronouncement made again and again in the Gospels to indicate that a miracle had taken place—someone has received sight, someone can walk. In this case a woman was forgiven and freed to go in peace.

God is interested in all sides of us. Because we are engaged in significant work, we must surely say that God is particularly interested in the spiritual healing that it brings to us. This healing begins with the miracle of forgiveness.

Reflecting and Recording

Can you imagine what would happen if today a woman from the streets fell at your feet, washed them with her tears, and wiped them with her hair? What might you do?

Prayer

We wouldn't be so arrogant, dear Jesus, to think we need just a little bit of forgiveness, nor would we be so wrong as to judge others and think them greater sinners than we are. We're all sinners, and here we are in your presence to express our devotion and our love. Let our actions reflect hearts that are fully devoted to you and your love. Let our deeds tell the world that we adore you and worship you. We've all gone astray. We've all missed the mark. Dear Jesus, please forgive us. Amen.

DAY FIVE: PUTTING OURSELVES IN THE ROOM

Part of learning the Scriptures in our hearts and then following them in our lives is to imagine ourselves as part of the story. Imagine the room where Jesus was sitting with the Pharisees. Imagine the light, the food, the furniture, and all the actions taking place. Now, if you can, try to put yourself into that scene. Here is my best try:

I wonder if anyone knew what it took for the woman to wash Jesus' feet, if they had any idea what she was really doing when she walked into their midst and knelt down.

She had crossed what felt like a mountain before she arrived there. Afterwards, she never regretted doing it; she only wished they had known her heart and realized that her intentions were as pure as the oil—that oil that they would later say could have been sold to feed the hungry. Most of the people in the room never understood how long she had held onto the oil and therefore how valuable it really was, as if it had any true worth before the moment she used it to wash his feet.

As she entered the room, she thought about the small vial she carried in the pouch that hung inside her apron. She paused just a moment before she went in and wondered if she could go through with her idea. She had carried the oil with her for so long that she scarcely remembered where she had gotten it. She remembered that she had received it when she was young, from a man who told sweet lies. He had said that it was valuable and that it was full of rich and fragrant aromas.

She had never been sure of what to do with the oil; and so as she moved from place to place, she carried it with her, knowing that, like wine, it would get better. And so it sat for years and became a silent testimony to her life. Several years ago, she had added olive leaves that were given to her by a dear friend. She added spice with a scent of cloves and just a touch of rosemary. The oil had seen her through death and birth, had witnessed love and anger, had helped her through times when she longed to be special and carry the fragrance of grace.

But something had changed for her, and she needed to acknowledge it in some way. She wanted to do something terribly kind and gentle for a person who had reminded her that she was worthy and good. And so an idea was born in her heart to offer him this precious oil that no one even knew she had. She knew she couldn't wrap it and hand it to him; he might think it was intended for someone else. She had to do something with it. She couldn't bathe him in it, as she wanted to, telling everyone in the room how kind and wonderful he had been and how he had convinced her that love was, in the end, the salvation of all. Then they would know for sure that she harbored some confused feelings about where humanity stops and God begins.

From nowhere, it seemed, a thought crept into her head that she could wash his feet in the oil. She could take this costly symbol and pour it over his worn and tired feet. She thought that made the most sense, because he would know what she meant and the others probably wouldn't understand. So she decided to do it—just walk in, thank him for everything, cleanse herself and him, and then walk out.

What she didn't expect was that when she knelt down and poured her past over his feet, she began to cry and could not stop. Her tears washed away even that sacred oil, so that the only thing left was the gift of her tears. She felt self-conscious; and so, trying to avoid everyone's eyes, she took her hair and even wiped those tears away. There was nothing left to do but hold the silence for another second, to let all the gratitude she felt come back to her. Then she fumbled with the jar and left the room.

The others never really got it. He defended her to the group; but as she thought about it later, she was not sure if he understood that what she did was to offer him the best of her so that he could see how beautiful he was.

The woman's feelings, as she poured out her life on Jesus' feet, were later captured perfectly by nineteenth-century hymn writer, Frances R. Havergal:

Take My Life, and Let It Be

Take my life, and let it be
consecrated, Lord, to thee.
Take my moments and my days;
let them flow in ceaseless praise.
Take my hands, and let them move
at the impulse of thy love.
Take my feet, and let them be
swift and beautiful for thee.

Take my voice, and let me sing
always, only, for my King.
Take my lips, and let them be
filled with messages from thee.
Take my silver and my gold;
not a mite would I withhold.
Take my intellect, and use
every power as thou shalt choose.

Take my will, and make it thine;
it shall be no longer mine.
Take my heart, it is thine own;
it shall be thy royal throne.
Take my love, my Lord, I pour
at thy feet its treasure-store.
Take myself, and I will be
ever, only, all for thee.

Frances Ridley Havergal (1873)

Reflecting and Recording

Can you write a short story or poem expressing your gratitude to God?

Prayer

O God, the greatness and beauty of whose work surround us from daybreak to sunset, so fill our imaginations, so fill our thoughts that we are left with nothing but praise on our lips as we fall asleep this night. Amen.

DAY SIX: SUMMING IT UP

John 15:11-17

I have said these things to you so that my joy may be in you,
and that your joy may be complete. This is my commandment,
that you love one another as I have loved you. No one has greater love
than this, to lay down one's life for one's friends. You are my friends
if you do what I command you. I do not call you servants any longer,
because the servant does not know what the master is doing;
but I have called you friends, because I have made known to you
everything that I have heard from my Father. You did not choose me
but I chose you. And I appointed you to go and bear fruit, fruit that will last,
so that the Father will give you whatever you ask him in my name.
I am giving you these commands so that you may love one another.

The Scripture on this last day of readings grounds us again in the love of Jesus as expressed in John. The words offer us assurance that all we are doing and studying is so that our joy may be in our Lord and may be complete. What greater goal could we strive for in our lives? This passage reminds us that first God chose us, and then we try to return that honor all the days of our lives. We honor God most truly by loving our brothers and sisters. Jesus says we are to love them so much that we are willing to lay down our lives for them. When we live like this, we demonstrate that we truly are friends of Jesus, walking in his path and following him in humility and gratitude.

We began this study by asking if it were possible to find balance in our faith between our hearts and minds. The premise was that there is a place where duty and devotion can balance one another perfectly and we can live in peace. But as the weeks progressed and we looked at the lives of women such as Mary and Martha, Lydia, Jesus' mother, the Canaanite woman, Mary Magdalene, Priscilla, and others, we didn't find balance. What we found was women who were devoted and dutiful, who loved fiercely, whose actions preached poetically. What we found were Scriptures saying that we must love God with all our hearts and minds. Our search did not answer our original question but led to a new place of understanding. We do not find faith by trying to balance an equal amount of duty on one hand and devotion on the other. If that were the formula, then we would always feel the push and pull of other people and our own responsibilities.

By the fourth week, I knew that the issue of balance was fading into the background. The question had changed from "How can we have balance?" to "How can we live faithfully?"

It seems to me that there are two reasons the question changed. First, we strive for balance because we desire peace. But the only way to live peacefully in our faith is not through balance but through complete surrender. The only way to feel peaceful is by being obedient to the will of God. The Gospels say that in order to save our lives, we must lose them and be completely devoted. To me, that does not sound like a recipe for balance.

The second reason the question changed was because balance began to feel like a compromise brought on by fear of truly believing the message of the gospel. That fear leads us away from love and from God; it will never bring us peace. If we are faithful, ultimately we will love God so much that we will be willing to lay down our lives for our brothers and sisters, and that is not such a great answer for those of us looking for balance.

None of this prevents balance from being a possibility; it's just not the goal. Love is the goal, and balance may be a byproduct. We may, like Mary Magdalene and the Canaanite woman, feel more balance because we no longer seem inadequate, experience pressure to live others' expectations of us, are haunted by our past, or worry about materialistic things. We may, like the mother of Jesus, feel more balance because we no longer question what to do or where to go but trust that God is leading us always. We may, like Lydia, feel more balance because we allow our faith to come first and never apologize for who we are or what gifts we possess. We may, like Mary and Martha, feel more balanced because we are free to bring our frustrations and gratitude to the feet of the Lord and know that we will be heard. We may feel more balance because we know our hearts and minds better after taking the time to study and be in prayer.

Whatever the journey has been like for you, please remember that all of us are struggling to know Scripture and the heart of God. I was attending a meeting about race relations at a local university when I met John Hope Franklin, a giant in that field. Eighty years old at that time, he had written several books that had influenced national opinions about race and was considered a father of the Civil Rights Movement. He was a friend of the founder of the university's race relations institute and had always served on its board.

When Franklin spoke about race relations that day, he began with these words: "I am still learning about race. . . ." Those words hit me hard. What a beautiful and open man he was. He could have started by saying, "Now, many of you think that I am wise . . . " or "In the last ten books I have written . . ."; but instead he was humble and willing to learn from others. I pray that I am always that open to new learning, especially in my faith. If I begin another study like this one and don't learn along the way or change my path, I am not truly listening to God.

It is important that all of us who have been thinking about balancing duty and devotion give love the very last word. Without love, all that we do is hollow, says Paul; with love, everything is redeemed, says our Lord.

Thank you so much for allowing me to spend this time reflecting with you, remembering the great women of Scriptures and thinking about the people who have taught me so much about faith. My prayer for each of you is to feel truly beloved by a God who knows you as God's child and will be with you all the days of your life, so that you can serve God every day and in the age to come. May God's joy be complete in you; and may the peace of God, which passes all understanding, keep your heart and mind in the knowledge and love of God, and in the Son, Jesus Christ our Lord.

Reflecting and Recording

What is the one thing you will remember most clearly from this Bible study series?

Prayer

A Franciscan Blessing

May God bless you with discomfort at easy answers, half-truths,
and superficial relationships, so that you may live deep within your heart.

May God bless you with anger at injustice, oppression, and exploitation
of people, so that you may work for justice, freedom, and peace.

May God bless you with tears to shed for those who suffer from pain,
rejection, starvation, and war, so that you may reach out your hand
to comfort them and to turn their pain into joy.

And may God bless you with enough foolishness to believe
that you can make a difference in this world,
so that you can do what others claim cannot be done.
Amen.

DAY SEVEN: PREPARING FOR GROUP DISCUSSION

What about your faith has changed during this study? What would you have liked to do differently? Will you keep up the practice of praying daily as part of a Scripture study?

Benediction

The sun begins the procession in a deep orange chasuble
as the frogs and crickets begin the opening hymn.
The thistle genuflects reverently as the leaves
rustle to find their place.

The spring-fed lake reflects on the world,
and is ready to accept the born-again dragonflies
that have heard the call.

The harmonies of the cardinals, sparrows,
and occasional crow offer the praise,
as creation begins its communion with the moon.

And just as the sun dips beneath the shroud of trees that covers it
and turns the day to memory,
a barred owl calls out the benediction.

Let creation, which passes all understanding,
keep your heart and mind in the knowledge and love of God.
Let the dirt you are made from join in the last chorus,
and let the water that flows through your veins give thanks.

Bibliography

Achtemeier, Paul J., ed., *HarperCollins Bible Dictionary*, HarperSanFrancisco, 1985.

Brown, Raymond Edward, Joseph A. Fitzmyer and Roland E. Murphy, eds., *The New Jerome Biblical Commentary*, Collegeville, Minnesota: Liturgical Press, 1992.

Chadwick, Patricia, "Mary Magdalene: Faithful Friend," *History's Women* (an online magazine, *www.historyswomen.com*).

Chittister, Joan, *The Friendship of Women: A Spiritual Tradition*, Franklin, Wisconsin: Sheed and Ward Publishing, 2000.

Deen, Edith, *All of the Women of the Bible*, New York: Harper and Brothers Publishers, 1955.

Ellsberg, Robert, ed., *Dorothy Day: Selected Writings*, London: Orbis, 1992.

Foster, Richard and James Bryan Smith, eds. *Devotional Classics*, HarperSanFrancisco,1993.

Fuchs, Lucy, *We Were There: Women in the New Testament*, New York: Alba House, 1993.

Klug, Lyn, *Soul Weavings: A Gathering of Women's Prayers*, Minneapolis: Augsburg Fortress, 1996.

Llewelyn, Robert, ed. *The Joy of the Saints,*
    London: Darton, Longman and Todd, 1988.

Meyers, Carol. ed., *Women in Scripture,*
    Grand Rapids, Michigan: Wm. Eerdmans, 2001.

Parks, Rosa, *Quiet Strength: The Faith, the Hope, and the Heart of a Woman
    Who Changed a Nation,* Grand Rapids, Michigan: Zondervan, 1994.

Picknett, Lynn, *Mary Magdalene: Christianity's Hidden Goddess,*
    New York: Carroll and Graf Publishers, 2003.

Stewart, Dorothy, compiler, *Women of Prayer: An Anthology of Everyday Prayers
    from Women Around the World,* Chicago: Loyola Press, 1999.